SOTHIS PRESS

Sothis Press aims to completely reimagine the public domain book with an emphasis on universal access to captivatingly designed print editions. We believe that technology will enable every single book ever published to be perpetually accessible in beautiful print form. Sothis is beauty in ubiquity.

www.sothis.press
1 Waterhouse Square, London, ECIN 2ST

A Manual for Notaries Public, Justices of the Peace

And Their Employers in Massachusetts

James T. Keen

SOTHIS PRESS

ISBN 978-1-0368-0990-4

A Manual for Notaries Public, Justices of the Peace is in the public domain.

This edition is published by Sothis Press © 2023. The company is registered in England and Wales. The Company Number is 14900389.

PREFACE.

The powers and duties of notaries public and of justices of the peace in Massachusetts have been so materially changed by recent legislation that a new guide book for such officers is not only a convenience but a necessity. This work, so far as it relates to Justices, is, to some extent, founded on W. M. Seavey's excellent "Manual for Notaries and Justices." This by permission.

The most important duties of notaries public relate to the protest of commercial paper, and to the noting and extending of marine protests. Formerly, the law of commercial paper was to be found, for the most part, in the decisions of the Supreme Judicial Court of Massachusetts, and in the decisions of the courts of last resort of the United States, of the several other States, and of England. But by Acts of 1898, Chapter 533, incorporated in the Revised Laws, Chapter 73, "Of Money and Negotiable Instruments," the law of commercial paper has been made (to a great degree) statutory. In any case, however, not therein provided for, resort must still be had to the law merchant; *i. e.* the law of bills, notes, and checks apart from statute.

A clear knowledge of the duties of notaries public relating to the protest of commercial paper is vital to every notary. To what extent these duties have been changed by the Act referred to may be gathered from the following pages. Constant reference has been made to Bigelow on "Bills and Notes," a work which has been truly styled a legal classic.

It is a curious fact that American text writers on "Notaries" have usually failed to treat of the noting and extending of marine protests, the most lucrative act the notary is called upon to perform. This work involves a knowledge of laws and customs unfamiliar to the average attorney, and unknown to the ordinary notary. The author has endeavored to rob this branch of the notarial office of its mystery by stating the law relating to marine protests, the customs of merchants, mariners, and average adjusters relating thereto as declared by these persons, and as interpreted in the decisions of the Admiralty Courts, and by presenting accurate, approved forms of marine protests in daily use at the port of Boston. Able assistance has been afforded by Mr. George M. Ameridge, Secretary of the Boston Board of Marine Underwriters, and by Messrs. Theodore W. and Christopher Gore, average adjusters.

The duties and privileges of justices of the peace have been carefully stated, and recent changes in the scope of their authority noted. It will be seen that the number of justices of the peace who may solemnize marriage has recently been greatly abridged; and the rights of such officers to perform many other acts seriously modified.

Important editorial assistance has been rendered by Mr. Arthur P. Gay, of the Boston Bar, who has critically examined the manuscript. Valuable suggestions touching the protest of commercial paper have been received from Mr. J. T. Auerbach, of the Boston Bar.

JAMES TOWER KEEN.

6, Beacon Street, Boston.

TABLE OF CONTENTS.

PART I.

NOTARIES PUBLIC.

PART II.

JUSTICES OF THE PEACE,

AND

SPECIAL COMMISSIONERS.

CHAPTER I.

CHAPTER II.

CHAPTER III.

CHAPTER IV.

CHAPTER V.

CHAPTER VI.

CHAPTER VII.

TABLE OF CASES.

PART I.

NOTARIES PUBLIC.

PART I.

NOTARIES PUBLIC.

CHAPTER I.

ORIGIN OF THE OFFICE OF NOTARY PUBLIC.

§ 1. A notary, *registrarius*, *actuarius*, *scrinarius*, was in early times a scribe that only took *notes* or minutes, and made short drafts of writings and other instruments, both public and private.[1] Cranstoun tells us that these scribes, with varying functions, practised not only among the ancient Jews, but in Egypt, Greece, and Rome. In the last century of the Roman republic, and probably in the days of Cicero, Roman scribes devised systems of short hand; and some of them, instead of using alphabetical letters, employed *notae*, or arbitrary signs of abbreviation for words in common use. The scribe who used this method was called *notarius*. Hence "notary" originally signified "a short-hand writer."[2] The office of notary public has been

[1] Byles on Bills, 262.

[2] Brooke's Notary [6th Ed. ch. 1, by Cranstoun], 2.

known to the majority of the Christian nations for hundreds of years. In those countries which have taken the Roman law as the basis of their legal system, the duties of notaries public are of the greatest importance and very varied in their character, while in countries like the United States and England, which use the common law of England, the duties are much more limited. As notaries public are found in nearly all parts of the civilized world, they were formerly of very great use to shipmasters, merchants, and other persons having dealings with foreign nations, in attesting writings and in certifying to acts done by them or in their presence, which might require to be proved in foreign countries. Now, however, the office is of less importance in its international relations than it was formerly. At the present time states and countries have very generally defined by statutes the majority of the acts which notaries may perform, the effect of these acts and the uses which may be made of notarial certificates within their respective jurisdictions.

§ 2. When notaries were first introduced into England, it is impossible to say. During the reign of Edward the Confessor, however, whilst Reinbald was Chancellor, certain manors and lands were granted by the King to the Abbot of Westminster by charter which was written and attested by one Swardius, a notary. In a deed by King John, dated 1199, one Master Philip, a notary of the

Pope, was granted thirty marks of silver annually, until the King could provide him with an ecclesiastical benefice. These were papal and imperial notaries, whose visits to England up to that time were rare. In 1237 when Cardinal Otho, a papal legate, was invited to England by Henry III., and held a council at St. Paul's, in London, "to strengthen and reform the state of the Church in England," it was declared that there were no notaries public then practising in England. But in 1292 (20 Edward I.), Master John Bush, a notary public of London, received a fee of 100*s*. from the Exchequer in compensation for his labor in transcribing and reducing into a public form certain papal bulls, and for expenses incurred in journeying to the King at Ambresbury upon the same business. Hence we may conclude that notaries public first practised in England at some time between 1237 and 1292. In the reign of Edward II., during the great controversy with Rome, foreign notaries, papal and imperial, were forbidden to practise in England.[1] It is clear that in England notaries public were formerly appointed by the authority of the Pope of Rome; but since the passage of the Statute of 25 Hen. VIII., ch. 21, they have been appointed by the Archbishop of Canterbury, who in the instrument of appointment decrees, "that full faith be given, as well in as out of judgment, to the instruments by them to be

[1] Brooke's Notary, 10, 11, 12.

made." This appointment is also registered and subscribed by the clerk of His Majesty for faculties in chancery. Thus notaries are at this day public officers of the civil and canon law.[1]

§ 3. In Massachusetts, under the Charter of the Colony of Massachusetts Bay, notaries public were elected by the General Court, which prescribed the oath to be taken by them and some of their duties and established their fees and the form of their seals, which were engraved at the expense of the Colony. They were also exempted from militia service.

§ 4. Notaries public were not mentioned in the Province Charter, but it appears that until the year 1720 they were appointed by the Governor and Council, in the same manner as judicial officers were appointed. In that year the House of Representatives contended that notaries public should be elected by the General Court, in accordance with the clause in the Charter which granted power to that Court "to name and settle annually all civil officers" except those otherwise provided for in the Charter, subject to the approbation of the Governor. This claim was conceded, and afterwards notaries public were elected by the Council and House of Representatives in concurrence. No Provincial statute was passed which defined any of the duties of notaries public, although their fees were established by statute. Apparently the

[1] Byles on Bills, 262.

only duties which they performed under the Province Charter were those which were attached to the office by custom.

§ 5. The Constitution of the Commonwealth as originally adopted provided that notaries public should be chosen annually by joint ballot of the Senators and Representatives in one room; but this was changed by the Fourth Amendment to the Constitution, so that now notaries are appointed by the Governor in the same manner as judicial officers are appointed, and they hold their offices for seven years, unless sooner removed by the Governor, with the consent of the Council, upon the address of both houses of the legislature.

§ 6. At the present time notaries public in this Commonwealth are empowered by statute to perform various acts in addition to the presentment and protest of foreign bills of exchange and the noting and extending of marine protests, which are attached to the office of notary public by custom.[1]

[1] Opinion of the Justices, 150 Mass. 586; Seavey's Manual for Notaries and Justices, 1.

CHAPTER II.

METHOD OF APPOINTMENT.

§ 7. Notaries public are appointed by the Governor in the same manner as judicial officers are appointed, and hold their offices during seven years, unless sooner removed by the Governor, with the consent of the Council, upon the address of both houses of the legislature.[1] They have jurisdiction and the right to act in any and all the counties of the Commonwealth.

§ 8. There is no statute prescribing the qualifications which persons must have to be appointed notaries public. The requisites which are established by custom are that the applicant for the office of notary public must be a citizen of the United States, a resident of Massachusetts, more than twenty-one years of age, and of high standing and character. A woman is not eligible for the office,[2] and a statute declaring her eligible would be unconstitutional.[3]

[1] Mass. Const. Amend., Art. IV.

[2] Opinion of the Justices, 150 Mass. 586.

[3] Opinion of the Justices, 165 Mass. 599.

§ 9. A blank application similar to the following form may be obtained at the office of the Secretary of State. As applications for the office of notary public are scrutinized very carefully, the strongest possible reasons should be alleged to show the necessity for the appointment, and the applicant should secure the names of prominent men as signatures to the application, so that, if need be, they could urge the appointment in person.

Form of Application for the Office of Notary Public.

COMMONWEALTH OF MASSACHUSETTS.

TO HIS EXCELLENCY THE GOVERNOR:

I hereby petition for appointment to the office of

NOTARY PUBLIC

FOR THE COMMONWEALTH OF MASSACHUSETTS.

Residence [1] ....

Business address [2] ....

Occupation ....

I was born in .... Age ....

I desire the appointment for the following reasons: [state the best reasons possible]

(Sign here.) ....

(The above blank must be filled out by the applicant and no one else.)

We certify that we are personally acquainted with the above-named applicant and consider him a man of

[1] Give city or town. [2] Give street and number.

high standing and character and in every way fitted to be commissioned a Notary Public.

....

....

Dated this..
day of........................190 .

(This certificate must be signed by at least two well-known persons.)

If the applicant was born in a foreign country, he must furnish proof that he is a citizen of the United States.

§ 10. When the blanks in the application have been suitably filled, it must be deposited in the executive office at the State House. The applicant will be notified in due season, should his application be acted upon favorably.

§ 11. A person appointed by the Governor to the office of notary public shall be notified of his appointment by the Secretary of the Commonwealth and his commission delivered to him, and if he does not, within three months after the date of such appointment, take and subscribe the oaths of office, his appointment shall be void, and the Secretary shall forthwith notify him thereof and require him to return his commission, and shall also certify said facts to the Governor.[1]

§ 12. Before the delivery of a commission to a person appointed notary public he shall pay to the Secretary of the Commonwealth a fee of five dollars.[2]

[1] R. L. ch. 18, § 8. [2] R. L. ch. 18, § 9.

§ 13. The following oath shall be taken by every person appointed to the office of notary public, before he shall enter on the duties of his office, to wit: —

"I, A. B., do solemnly swear, that I will bear true faith and allegiance to the Commonwealth of Massachusetts, and will support the Constitution thereof. So help me, God."

Provided, That when any person shall be of the denomination called Quakers, and shall decline taking said oath, he shall make his affirmation in the foregoing form, omitting the word "swear," and inserting, instead thereof, the word "affirm," and omitting the words "So help me, God," and subjoining, instead thereof, the words, "This I do under the pains and penalties of perjury." [1]

EXPIRATION OF APPOINTMENT.

§ 14. The Secretary of the Commonwealth shall send by mail to every notary public a notice of the time of the expiration of his commission, not more than thirty nor less than fourteen days before such expiration.[2]

§ 15. Whoever presumes to act as a notary public after the expiration of his commission, and after receiving notice of such expiration, shall be punished by fine of not less than one hundred nor more than five hundred dollars.[3]

[1] Mass. Const. Amend., Art. VI.

[2] R. L. ch. 5, § 8. [3] R. L. ch. 210, § 34.

§ 16. On the death, resignation or removal from office of a notary public, his records and official papers shall be deposited in the office of the clerk of the courts in the county in which he resided, or, if he resided in the county of Suffolk, in the office of the clerk of the Superior Court of said county for Civil Business.[1]

§ 17. A notary public who neglects for three months after his resignation or removal from office so to deposit his records and official papers, or the executor or administrator of a deceased notary who neglects for three months after his acceptance of such office so to deposit such records and official papers of the deceased which come into his hands shall forfeit not more than five hundred dollars.[2]

§ 18. Whoever knowingly destroys, defaces, or conceals the records or official papers of a notary public shall forfeit a sum not exceeding one thousand dollars, and be liable in damages to any party injured thereby.[3]

SEALS.

§ 19. By custom, a notary public must have an official seal, and copies of his records must be certified under his seal.[4] The seal used by notaries public in this Commonwealth consists of an impression containing the name of the notary and

[1] R. L. ch. 17, § 2. [2] R. L. ch. 17, § 3.

[3] R. L. ch. 17, § 4.

[4] Opinion of the Justices, 150 Mass. 586 at 589.

the designation of his office, made upon the paper which is to receive the seal by means of a stamp.

§ 20. Judicial notice is taken of the seal of a notary public as an officer recognized by the commercial world.[1] His signature to an instrument going to a foreign country or to another state, must often be authenticated in some way, usually in the case of a foreign country by the consul of that country; but in case of a protest made upon the non-acceptance or non-payment of commercial paper, the notarial seal is sufficient in itself, without further authentication.[2]

[1] 1 Greenl. Evid., 15th ed., § 5. Hutcheon *v.* Mannington, 6 Ves. 823.

[2] Orr *v.* Lacy, 4 McLean (U. S.), 243; Pierce *v.* Indseth, 106 U. S. 546. Seavey's Manual for Notaries and Justices, Chapter II.

CHAPTER III.

POWERS APART FROM STATUTE.

PART I.

THE PROTEST OF COMMERCIAL PAPER,

UNDER REVISED LAWS, CHAPTER 73,

"*Of Money and Negotiable Instruments.*"[1]

HISTORICAL.

§ 21. One important branch of a notary's practice is connected with bills of exchange and promissory notes, the history of which is thus ably summarized by Brooke in his work on "The Office and Practice of a Notary in England."[2]

"The introduction and use of bills of exchange in England were founded on the practice of merchants, and gradually acquired the force of a custom. There is no authentic record of the first introduction of bills into England. They are referred to in the statute of

[1] This Act is designated in the following pages simply as "The Statute." This for the sake of brevity.

[2] Brooke's Notary, 70 [6th edition].

3 Rich. II. as a means of conveying money out of the realm, though not as a process in use amongst English merchants. Promissory notes payable to bearer, or to a man and his assigns, were known in England in the time of Edward IV., and there is no doubt that both bills and notes were used in England during the fifteenth and sixteenth centuries. The earliest reported case, however, on the subject is that of Martin *v.* Boure, in Croke's reports, in the first year of the reign of James I.[1] About that time the practice of making bills payable to *order* and transferring them by indorsement, arose. In the time of Holt, C. J., a conflict arose between him and the merchants as to the negotiability of promissory notes. The Chief Justice held that they were not negotiable by indorsement or delivery. The inconvenience to trade arising from this decision led to the passing of 3 & 4 Anne, ch. 8, whereby promissory notes were made capable of being assigned by indorsement, or made payable to bearer and such assignment, which had been customary for some time amongst merchants, was rendered valid beyond all question. Foreign bills of exchange between English and foreign merchants were in use in England long before inland bills came into existence."

§ 22. Until 1882, the law in England relating to bills, notes, and checks was contained in numerous cases and Acts of Parliament, but in that year was passed the "Bills of Exchange Act" (45 and 46 Vict. ch. 61), which was intended to codify and

[1] Cro. Jac. 6.

slightly change the existing law, and to repeal and reenact with modifications most of the statutes relating to those instruments. This act is, to a great extent, the basis of the statute in Massachusetts which treats of negotiable instruments and their protest by notaries public. The rules of the common law, however, including the law merchant, except so far as inconsistent with the express provisions of the statute, continue in force, and questions relating to bills that are not provided for by the statute, and have not been judicially decided, must still be determined by the usage of trade, and the application of the general principles of law.[1]

PROTEST DEFINED.

§ 23. When a foreign bill of exchange on its face so appearing is presented for acceptance or for payment, or when a foreign check so appearing is presented for payment, and such acceptance or payment is refused, the instrument is dishonored, and *must* be protested. This protest is a solemn declaration of the facts constituting dishonor, and is usually under the hand and seal of a notary public. Its object is to fix the liability of parties not primarily liable on the paper.

§ 24. By statute, inland bills and checks, and foreign and inland promissory notes *may* be protested, but protest is not required.

[1] Brooke's Notary, 71.

DEGREE OF KNOWLEDGE REQUIRED IN PROTESTING PAPER.

§ 25. The notary public who is called upon to make protest need not have a broad knowledge of the law of commercial paper. Ordinarily he is safe if he obeys his employer's orders. Thus, where a bill was delivered to a notary with directions to protest it on a certain day, which was the wrong day, the notary was held not to be liable because he acted on the erroneous instructions. He is not presumed to be a lawyer who is to revise or reverse the decision of his employer as to the character of the paper put into his hands, or as to when it falls due. It is the notary's duty to make protest, not to give legal advice.[1]

§ 26. A notary public should, however, be able to distinguish between the different kinds of commercial paper, since in his certificate of protest he states what kind of paper he has protested. While, therefore, the rigid requirements of his office do not oblige him to know whether or not there are present in the instrument to be protested *all* the elements necessary to constitute it commercial paper, nevertheless an understanding of some of the technical terms used in connection therewith may be of great convenience.

[1] Commercial Bank *v.* Varnum, 49 N. Y. 269.

TERMS DEFINED.

(*a*) *Paper*.

§ 27. Commercial paper, as here treated, consists of negotiable promissory notes, bills of exchange, and checks. A promissory note is a written promise, and a bill of exchange a written order upon a person, to pay to a certain person or order, or to the order of a certain person, or to bearer, a certain sum of money, absolutely. A check is a written order upon a bank or banker to pay on demand (otherwise as in the case of a note or bill). "Draft" is a term of convenience, signifying usually a bill, sometimes a check.[1]

§ 28. A negotiable instrument is one which conforms to the following requisites: (1) It must be in writing and signed by the maker or drawer; (2) it must contain an unconditional promise or order to pay a sum certain in money; (3) it must be payable on demand, or at a fixed or determinable future time; (4) it must be payable to order or to bearer; and (5) where an instrument is addressed to a drawee, he must be named or otherwise indicated therein with reasonable certainty.[2] *Some* of these terms themselves must be explained.

(1) "Writing." To constitute commercial paper, not only must there be a writing, but the whole engagement must be in writing, and all the terms

[1] Big. Bills and Notes, 11, 12.   [2] R. L. ch. 73, § 18.

necessary to constitute it a bill, note, or check must be found within the four corners of the piece of paper on which it is written. Thus a promise to pay one's debt would not be a promissory note, since resort must be had to external evidence to determine the amount payable. The instrument may be written with ink or pencil, and upon any material firm enough of itself to hold the writing.[1] It must be "signed" (and by the Statute may or may not be under seal, although by the law merchant paper bearing a seal was not negotiable).[2] But any party may sign with his mark though able to write his name, and with the same effect in law as if he had written his signature. If the party's name is not signed, the holder has to show that what the party did write was intended for a signature.[3]

(2) The promise must be "unconditional," not depending on a condition or contingency. For example: "One month after date I promise to pay A. or order $1,000, out of the net proceeds of ore to be obtained from the mine in the lot of land this day conveyed to me by B;"[4] or, "Due K. $1,000 when he is twenty-one years of age;"[5] or, "At sight after the arrival and discharge of coal per brig G. pay to the order of myself $1,500, value

[1] Big. Bills and Notes, 20, 21.
[2] Big. Bills and Notes, 10.
[3] Big. Bills and Notes, 38; Bliss *v.* Johnson, 162 Mass. 323.
[4] Worden *v.* Dodge, 4 Denio, 159.
[5] Kelley *v.* Hemingway, 13 Ill. 604.

received."[1] Clearly these are not promises or orders to pay absolutely, and hence not negotiable instruments. For perhaps the mine will never yield sufficient ore, or the boy attain the age of twenty-one, or the brig arrive and be discharged.[2] These are all contingent events.

Further, the paper must be payable in "money." "Money" is that which by law is tenderable for debt. The money of account in this Commonwealth is the dollar, cent, and mill.[3] Hence an instrument, "I promise to pay A. or order $140, in carpenter's work," is not a promissory note.[4]

Further, the sum payable must be "certain."[5] Thus, "Two years from date, for value received, we or either of us promise to pay W. or bearer $60, with use; said W. agrees that if $50 be paid on the first day of January, 1843, it shall cancel this note." This is not a promissory note.[6]

(3) The instrument "must be payable on *demand*, or at a fixed or *determinable future time*." Paper is payable on *demand* (*a*) where it is expressed to be payable on demand, at sight, or on presentation; or (*b*) if no time for payment is expressed, (as in the case of a common check):[7] it is payable at a *determinable future time* if it is expressed to be payable

[1] Grant *v.* Wood, 12 Gray, 220.

[2] Big. Bills and Notes, 32.

[3] R. L. ch. 73, § 1.

[4] Big. Bills and Notes, 27; Quinby *v.* Merritt, 11 Humph. 439.

[5] Big. Bills and Notes, 29; R. L. ch. 73, § 18.

[6] Fralick *v.* Norton, 2 Mich. 130.

[7] R. L. ch. 73, § 24.

(*a*) at a fixed period after date or sight; (*b*) on or before a fixed or determinable time specified in the instrument; or (*c*) on or at a fixed period after the occurrence of a specified event which is certain to happen, though the time of happening be uncertain,[1] (as, for example, a note payable a certain number of days after the death of the maker).[2] We have seen that an instrument payable on a contingency is not negotiable, and the happening of the event does not cure the defect.

(4) To be negotiable, and hence liable to come to the attention of the notary, the instrument must be payable "to order" or "to bearer," in terms or in plain meaning.

(5) So where the instrument is addressed to a drawee, he must be "named *or otherwise indicated* therein with reasonable certainty." For a bill of exchange is in its original a letter.[3] Thus, where a bill was made payable at "No. 1, Wilmot Street, opposite the Lamb, Bethnal Green, London," without mentioning the drawee's name, and the defendant accepted it, he was not allowed to make the objection, the bill "being directed to a particular place, which could only mean to the person who resided there."[4] So a bill may be directed to the drawee himself, though it is, in that case, a note rather than a bill.[5]

[1] R. L. ch. 73, § 21.

[2] Carnwright *v.* Gray, 127 N. Y. 92.

[3] Byles on Bills, 89.

[4] Gray *v.* Milner, 8 Taunt. 739.

[5] Byles on Bills, 90.

(*b*) *Parties.*

§ 29. The person who executes a promissory note is called the maker, not the drawer; the person who executes a bill of exchange is called the drawer, not the maker; and the person who executes a check is generally called the drawer, sometimes the maker. The person to whom, by name, a note, a bill, or a check is payable, is called the payee; the person upon whom a bill or check is drawn (*i. e.* who is called upon to make payment) is called the drawee; and if the instrument is a bill, and he accepts it, he is known as the acceptor. When the payee, or other person, puts his name upon the paper, he is an indorser. The person to whom the paper is then or later passed is the indorsee or holder. Parties absolutely liable are called primary parties, and are said to be primarily liable. Other parties are called secondary parties, and are said to be secondarily liable.[1]

Having, therefore, found out what commercial paper is, what the parties thereto are called, and that their liability sometimes *may*, sometimes *must* be fixed by an act called protest, we naturally inquire

[1] Big. Bills and Notes, 12.

OF WHAT PAPER IS PROTEST A NECESSITY?

(*a*) As to Foreign Bills and Foreign Checks.

§ 30. The most important duties of notaries public relate to the protest of commercial paper, especially of foreign bills. These are bills purporting on their face not to be both drawn and payable within this Commonwealth;[1] for the several states of the United States are foreign to each other, so far as concerns the law of the protest of commercial paper.[2] Where a foreign bill appearing on its face to be such is dishonored by non-acceptance, it must be duly protested therefor, and where such a bill, not previously dishonored by non-acceptance, is dishonored by non-payment, it must be protested for non-payment. If it is not so protested, the drawer and indorsers are disharged.[3] A bill protested for non-acceptance may be subsequently protested for non-payment.[4]

§ 31. Moreover, if an action is brought on the bill, there is ordinarily but one means of proving its dishonor, and that is by the notarial protest if the certificate is in existence and obtainable. It cannot be shown by witnesses or in any other way;

[1] R. L. ch. 73, § 146, changing the law merchant, which made the residence of the drawer and drawee the test. Grimshaw *v.* Bender, 6 Mass. 156; Phœnix Bank *v.* Hussey, 12 Pick. 483.

[2] Bank of United States *v.* Daniel, 12 Pet. 32; Commercial Bank *v.* Varnum, 49 N. Y. 269.

[3] R. L. ch. 73, § 169.

[4] R. L. ch. 73, § 174.

nor can its deficiencies be made good by extrinsic evidence, however clear, whether the protest be for non-acceptance or non-payment.[1]

§ 32. A check is defined by the Statute as a bill of exchange drawn on a bank payable on demand.[2] The Statute declares that sections eighteen to two hundred twelve thereof inclusive, which apply to bills of exchange payable on demand, shall apply to checks as well, except as otherwise provided.[3] There is no section differentiating foreign bills from foreign checks respecting protest. Hence it seems that foreign checks must be protested.[4]

(*b*) Inland Bills, Inland Checks, and Notes.

§ 33. Of the protest of inland bills and notes and checks, the unwritten law merchant knows nothing, and hence, so far as the protest of such paper is proper, it must rest upon statute. Our Statute permits but does not require the protest of such paper.[5] Since checks and bills seem to stand on

[1] Big. Bills and Notes, 130, 131; Phœnix Bank *v.* Hussey, 12 Pick. 483; Ocean Bank *v.* Williams, 102 Mass. 141.

[2] R. L. ch. 73, § 202.

[3] R. L. ch. 73, § 202.

[4] "Where a statute provides for a protest of inland bills and promissory notes, a check would be embraced within the description of paper denominated inland bills of exchange, and might be protested in like manner. And if drawn in one state upon another, a protest would, doubtless, be necessary to charge an indorser, the check being, in that event, a species of foreign bill." Daniel, Neg. Instr. § 1600; Harker *v.* Anderson, 21 Wend. 372; M'Lean *v.* Clydesdale Banking Co., 9 Appeal Cases, 95.

[5] Big. Bills and Notes, 132.

the same footing, so far as regards the necessity for protest,[1] we may dismiss inland checks by saying that they fall within the same rule as inland bills, next discussed.

§ 34. An inland bill is one which is, or on its face purports to be, both drawn and payable within this Commonwealth. The protest by a notary of inland bills and hence of inland checks is an official act; for it is recognized by section thirteen of the Statute, which makes protest of these instruments *prima facie* evidence of dishonor, and by section thirty-one of chapter two hundred four of the Revised Laws, which provides fees for the protesting of such paper. Notes are also thus recognized by the Statute.[2]

It being clear what paper is entitled to protest, the logical question is as to the

METHOD OF PROTESTING.

§ 35. The usual course is for the holder of the instrument to make presentment and demand for acceptance, if acceptance is required, or for payment, and then in case of refusal to place the paper in the hands of a notary public, who makes presentment and demand again.[3] If such acceptance, or payment, as the case may be, is refused,

[1] R. L. ch. 73, § 202.
[2] R. L. ch. 73, § 13; ch. 204, § 31.
[3] Big. Bills and Notes, 124.

he will then protest the instrument, and he may and by requirement of custom will give notice to the parties sought to be held.

§ 36. In protesting a negotiable instrument, the notary will proceed with the following steps: first, the presentment of the instrument for acceptance or for payment and the demand for acceptance or for payment; second, the noting of the fact of the dishonor; third (by custom), the notices to the drawer and to the indorsers, of the fact of the dishonor; fourth, extending or drawing up the formal protest; and a fifth step might be added, *i. e.* the recording of the protest. We shall consider these several steps in detail, first explaining the terms.

1. PRESENTMENT AND DEMAND.

§ 37. Presentment and demand are separate and distinct steps, and the law requires both, or some equivalent or substitute. "Presentment is the act of handing over the paper to the maker, drawee, or acceptor, or at least of exhibiting it to him, with a view to payment or acceptance according to the case and the purpose; demand is a request upon the party, at the same time, to accept or pay, according to the case and the purpose." But in ordinary cases it is unnecessary to draw any distinction between presentment and demand, and the terms may be treated as one.[1]

[1] Big. Bills and Notes, 105.

§ 38. Presentment is of two kinds: (1) for acceptance, and (2) for payment. The former simply seeks the assent duly manifested by the drawee of a bill to be bound thereon. The latter requires payment of the paper.

(*a*) *When Necessary.*

1. For Acceptance.

§ 39. First, of presentment of bills for acceptance. (Notes, and ordinarily checks, require no acceptance.) This must be made (1) where the bill is payable after sight, or in any other case where presentment for acceptance is necessary to fix the maturity of the instrument; or (2) where a bill expressly stipulates that it shall be presented for acceptance; or (3) where the bill is drawn payable elsewhere than at the residence or place of business of the drawee. But in no other case is presentment for acceptance necessary in order to render any party to the bill liable.[1] Thus, a bill payable at a stated time after date need not be presented for acceptance.[2]

§ 40. Except as the Statute otherwise provides, the holder of a bill required as above to be presented for acceptance must present it for acceptance or negotiate it within a reasonable time, failing which the drawer and all indorsers are discharged.[3]

[1] R. L. ch. 73, § 160.

[2] Walker *v.* Stetson, 19 Ohio St. 400.

[3] R. L. ch. 73, § 161.

§ 41. But presentment for acceptance is excused and a bill may be treated as dishonored (1) where the drawee is dead or has absconded or is a fictitious person or one not having capacity to contract by bill; (2) where, after the exercise of reasonable diligence, presentment cannot be made; or (3) where although presentment has been irregular, acceptance has been refused on some other ground.[1]

2. For Payment.

§ 42. Second, of presentment for payment. This is not necessary in order to charge the person primarily liable on the instrument, *i. e.* the maker of a note, or the drawee of a bill or check. But except as the Statute otherwise provides, presentment for payment is necessary to charge the drawer and indorsers.[2]

§ 43. *When* does the Statute otherwise provide? Presentment for payment is not required to charge the drawer where he has no right to expect or require that the drawee or acceptor will pay the instrument; or to charge an indorser where the instrument was made or accepted for his accommodation, and he has no reason to expect that it will be paid if presented.[3] But neither the insolvency[4] nor the infancy[5] of a drawee or maker, nor the

[1] R. L. ch. 73, § 165.

[2] R. L. ch. 73, § 87.

[3] R. L. ch. 73, §§ 96, 97.

[4] Granite Bank *v.* Ayers, 16 Pick. 312.

[5] Wyman *v.* Adams, 12 Cush. 210.

fact that the paper is overdue when indorsed[1] is a sufficient reason for not making a demand for payment. So also presentment for payment is dispensed with (1) where, after the exercise of reasonable diligence, presentment cannot be made; (2) where the drawee is a fictitious person; (3) by waiver of presentment, express or implied,[2] as where the maker of a note not yet due assigns all his property to his indorser.[3] So when a bill is dishonored by non-acceptance, no presentment for payment is necessary.[4] We shall elsewhere consider excuses of delay.

Paper Payable at Bank.

§ 44. It is not necessary, in the first instance, to make an actual demand upon the party primarily liable, when a negotiable instrument is payable at a particular bank; enough that the paper is there at maturity, to the knowledge of the bank.[5] For it is the party's duty, when the paper becomes due, to go to the bank and pay.

§ 45. Presentment of such paper for payment must be made during banking hours, unless the person to make payment has no funds there to meet it at any time during the day, in which case presentment at any hour before the bank is closed

1 Cook *v.* Barnard, 18 Pick. 260.
2 R. L. ch. 73, § 99.
3 Bond *v.* Farnham, 5 Mass. 170.
4 R. L. ch. 73, § 168.
5 Chicopee Bank *v.* Philadelphia Bank, 8 Wall. (U. S. 641.

on that day is sufficient.[1] All parties are presumed to take notice of the usual hours at which the bank is open. After the expiration of those hours, the time for payment has expired, the maker is in default, and the note is dishonored.

§ 46. But this rule has no application to paper not payable at a bank, by its terms or by usage, and not placed in any bank for collection. Therefore a notice to the maker or drawer, to the effect that the instrument is unpaid, is of no effect to charge the indorser without a demand on the maker or drawee for payment, although the indorser knows he is insolvent and has absconded.[2]

§ 46 a. It may be instructive to state an example of "Paper payable at bank by usage." There is a usage in Boston whereby if a note is placed in a bank for collection a sufficient presentment is made if notice is given to the maker before the note falls due informing him of the date when the note is payable and asking him to come and pay it. Thus paper was so placed with the S. Bank of Boston for collection, and such notice given the maker. The note remained unpaid in the bank through banking hours of the last day of grace. It became material to determine whether or not the promisor had consented to this usage. Shaw, C. J., said, "If the promisor was a trader, and accustomed to transact business at the bank,

[1] R. L. ch. 73, § 92; cf. Shepherd *v.* Chamberlain, 8 Gray, 225.
[2] Pierce *v.* Cate, 12 Cush. 190.

his consent to the general usage, which made such notice a good presentment and demand, might be shown; and indeed the usage has now been so universal in Boston, and so long continued, that slight evidence would be sufficient to prove acquiescence on the part of any trader, and thus make this established mode of demand a sufficient one."[1]

(b) *Who May Make.*

For Acceptance or Payment.

§ 47. Presentment for acceptance or payment should be made by the holder, or on his behalf, *i. e.* by his authorized agent. The party in possession of the bill is with ostensible legal title thereto, presumed to be the holder, and to have the right to make presentment for acceptance or payment.[2] The drawee may accept without risk, and if he refuse, the protest will inure to the benefit of the rightful holder.[3]

§ 48. Upon the death of the holder, presentment for payment should be made by his successor in title, *i. e.* by his executor or administrator. Of course a legatee could not require payment, although entitled to the money when paid. He is not the late holder's legal representative.[4]

1 Warren Bank *v.* Parker, 8 Gray, 221.

2 Daniel and Douglass, El. Neg. Instr. 165; Freeman *v.* Boynton, 7 Mass. 483.

3 Chitty on Bills (13 Am. ed.), 311.

4 Big. Bills and Notes, 124; Crist *v.* Crist, 1 Carter (Ind.), 570.

§ 49. There may be a double presentment. The first presentment is made by the holder of the paper or by his agent in the ordinary way. If, upon this first presentment, the paper is dishonored, and is to be protested, a second formal presentment must be made. By whom? By the law merchant, the notary himself must make this formal presentment and demand. Otherwise, his testimony in the protest would be hearsay merely, and would lack the very element of certainty which the certificate is designed to assure. Not even his clerk or deputy might perform this function for the notary, as it is to his official character that the law imputes the solemnity and sanction which are accorded his certificate.[1] To-day, under the Statute, protest of *bills of exchange* may be made by (1) a notary public; or (2) by any respectable resident of the place where the bill is dishonored, in the presence of two or more credible witnesses, thus making no theoretical distinction except in order of terms between a notary and "any respectable resident."[2] As a practical matter, protest of such paper is still usually made by a notary.

§ 50. As to promissory notes, the section of the Statute just discussed is silent; but these are governed by another section[3] which permits their pro-

[1] Daniel and Douglass, El. Neg. Instr. 228; Ocean Bank *v.* Williams, 102 Mass. 141.

[2] R. L. ch. 73, § 171; cf., Big. Bills and Notes, 125.

[3] R. L. ch. 73, § 13. See also ch. 204, § 31.

test by a notary. But suppose no notary can be found? Clearly we cannot apply the law merchant (*i. e.* the law of bills, notes, and checks apart from statute) which, though ordinarily requiring the act of a notary as essential to a valid protest, allows some other public officer or other respectable, disinterested person to act if no notary can be found to serve.[1] For the law merchant knows nothing of the protest of notes;[2] "it is only in relation to foreign bills of exchange that the protest of a foreign notary can be admitted in evidence, and notes . . . are certainly not bills of exchange."[3]

[1] Burke *v.* McKay, 2 How. 66; Todd *v.* M'Neal's Adm'r, 49 Ala. 273.

[2] City Bank *v.* Cutter, 3 Pick. 414. There are cases, however, tending to put foreign indorsed notes on a footing with foreign bills, so far as regards protest. Ticonic Bank *v.* Stackpole, 41 Maine, 302, [1856]. This doctrine is wrong. It was enunciated and hinted to be the law of Massachusetts in Carter *v.* Burley, 9 N. H. 558, which is cited in Ticonic Bank *v.* Stackpole, *supra*, but was explained in Smith *v.* Little, 10 N. H. 526. There it was said, "An indorsed note, though it may have a similitude to and an operation like a bill of exchange, is not one technically speaking; and it is not necessary to prove its dishonor by a protest, even where the maker and indorser reside in different governments." In Williams *v.* Putnam, 14 N. H. 540, [1844], Parker, C. J., who decided the two preceding cases, referring to the quoted language said, "But it by no means follows that it *may* not be proved in that way, although it is not necessary so to prove it." Daniel on Negotiable Instruments, § 928, states the true rule: "In strict law, it [the certificate of protest of a promissory note, although foreign] must be excluded" as evidence. "A general usage would probably be controlling." Burke *v.* McKay, 2 How. 66; Big. Bills and Notes, 132.

[3] Kirtland *v.* Wanzer, 2 Duer, 278, [1853].

Therefore protest of promissory notes if made at all must be made by a notary.

(c) *At What Time to be Made.*

1. For Acceptance.

§ 51. Presentment for acceptance must be made at a reasonable hour, on a business day and before the bill is overdue. A bill may be presented for acceptance on any day when a negotiable instrument may be presented for payment. When Saturday is not otherwise a legal holiday presentment for acceptance may be made before twelve o'clock noon on that day.[1] The words "legal holiday" include the twenty-second day of February, the nineteenth day of April, the thirtieth day of May, the fourth day of July, the first Monday of September, Thanksgiving day, and Christmas day, or the day following, when any of the four days first mentioned, or Christmas day, occurs on Sunday.[2]

§ 52. Delay in making presentment for acceptance is sometimes excused. Thus, where the holder of a bill drawn payable elsewhere than at the place of business or the residence of the drawee has not time with the exercise of reasonable diligence to present the bill for acceptance before presenting it for payment on the day that it falls due, the delay caused by presenting for acceptance be-

[1] R. L. ch. 73, § 163.

[2] R. L. ch. 8, § 5, cl. 9.

fore presenting for payment is excused and does not discharge the drawer and indorsers.[1]

2. For Payment.

§ 53. Every negotiable instrument is payable at the time fixed therein without grace, except that three days of grace are allowed upon a draft or bill of exchange made payable within this commonwealth at sight, unless there is an express stipulation to the contrary. When the day of maturity falls upon Sunday or a holiday the instrument is payable on the next succeeding business day. Instruments falling due or payable on Saturday are to be presented on the next succeeding business day, except that instruments payable on demand may, at the option of the holder, be presented for payment before twelve o'clock noon on Saturday, when that entire day is not a holiday.[2]

§ 54. Suppose paper is payable six months after a certain time: how shall the time be computed? Where the instrument is payable at a fixed period after date, after sight, or after the happening of a specified event, the time of payment is determined by excluding the day from which the time is to begin to run, and by including the date of payment.[3]

§ 55. There may, however, be a pardonable delay. Thus, delay in making presentment for payment is

[1] R. L. ch. 73, § 164.
[2] R. L. ch. 73, § 102.
[3] R. L. ch. 73, § 103.

excused when caused by circumstances beyond the holder's control, and not imputable to his default, misconduct, or negligence. For example, delay caused by the miscarriage of the mails.[1] But when the cause of delay ceases to operate, presentment must be made with reasonable diligence.[2]

§ 56. Where paper is payable on demand, presentment must be made within *a reasonable time* after its issue, except that in the case of a bill of exchange presentment for payment will be sufficient if made within *a reasonable time* after the last negotiation thereof.[3] In determining what is "a reasonable time" or "an unreasonable time," the Statute provides that regard must be had to the nature of the instrument, the usage of trade or business, if any, with respect to such instruments, and the facts of the particular case.[4]

§ 57. By the law merchant, the rule was well settled at an early date as to promissory notes payable on demand.[5] In Field *v.* Nickerson, 13 Mass. 131, the period of eight months was held not to be a reasonable time to make a demand to charge the indorser; and in Seaver *v.* Lincoln, 21 Pick. 267, where the demand was made in

[1] Windham Bank *v.* Norton, 22 Conn. 213; Pier *v.* Heinrichshoffen, 67 Mo. 163. See also Wylie *v.* Cotter, 170 Mass. 356.

[2] R. L. ch. 73, § 98.

[3] R. L. ch. 73, § 88; Acts 1898, ch. 533, § 197, reviving the law merchant of more than sixty years ago.

[4] R. L. ch. 73, § 209.

[5] Merritt *v.* Jackson, 181 Mass. 69.

seven days after the date of the note, it was held to be within due time. In Sylvester *v.* Crapo, 15 Pick. 92, a note that had remained unpaid for eleven months before it was negotiated, was held to be dishonored; and the shorter period of six months was, in Thompson *v.* Hale, 6 Pick. 259, held sufficient to subject it to the defence of a note overdue. On the other hand, a note indorsed seven days after its date was held, in Thurston *v.* M'Kown, 6 Mass. 428, to have been transferred in season to avoid any ground of defence arising from the equities between the original parties. In Ranger *v.* Cary, 1 Met. 369, it was held that a note payable on demand was not to be regarded as overdue, if indorsed within one month after its date. In Merritt *v.* Jackson, 181 Mass. 69, Lathrop, J., declared that in the absence of any evidence of usage of trade to bring it within the statutory definition of "reasonable time" above quoted, a demand on a promissory note payable on demand must be made within sixty days of the date in order to hold an indorser. So much for a definition of the phrase "reasonable time" in this branch of the law of commercial paper.

§ 58. The presentment must be "at a reasonable hour on a business day."[1] Except where paper is payable at bank, the holder has the whole day in which to present the same, subject to the limitation stated. What is "a reasonable hour" may

[1] R. L. ch. 73, § 89.

depend on the circumstances of the case. As late as nine o'clock in the evening has been held to be "a reasonable hour."[1] But payment should not be called for during the hours of rest, as, for instance, near midnight. The fact that the maker or acceptor has gone to bed early, perhaps because he is tired or sick, will not make the presentment improper. "The question whether a presentment is within reasonable time cannot be made to depend on the private and peculiar habits of the maker of a note, not known to the holder; but it must be determined by a consideration of the circumstances which, in ordinary cases, would render it reasonable or otherwise."[2] So the test of "a reasonable hour" may depend on locality. Thus, presentment upon a maker at his place of residence in a city at eight o'clock in the morning is too early;[3] while presentment so made in the country, at a farmer's house, would be reasonable.[4]

We have already considered paper payable at bank.

(*d*) *How and Where to be Made.*

1. For Acceptance.

§ 59. How? The proper manner of making a presentment of a bill of exchange for acceptance is

[1] Farnsworth *v.* Allen, 4 Gray, 453.
[2] Big. Bills and Notes, 122; Farnsworth *v.* Allen, 4 Gray, 453.
[3] Lunt *v.* Adams, 17 Maine, 230.
[4] Big. Bills and Notes, 123.

for the notary to exhibit the bill to the drawee or some person authorized to accept or refuse on his part and unequivocally to demand acceptance. If the party presenting does not produce the bill, the drawee may require him to do so, and decline to accept save by writing his name on its face; and then unless the holder produces it, the drawee cannot be charged with the penalties of non-acceptance.[1]

§ 60. If the bill is addressed to two or more not partners presentment must be made to them all, unless one is authorized to act for the rest, when presentment to him only suffices. Where the drawee is dead, presentment may be made to his personal representative. Where the drawee has been adjudged a bankrupt or an insolvent, or has made an assignment for creditors, presentment may be made to him or to his trustee or assignee.[2]

2. For Payment.

§ 61. How? Presentment for payment of a bill or note should be made by an actual exhibition of the instrument itself; or at least the demand of payment should be accompanied by some clear indication that the instrument is at hand, ready to be delivered, and such must actually be the case. Thus, a demand was held insufficient be-

[1] Fall River Union Bank *v.* Willard, 5 Met. 216.

[2] R. L. ch. 73, § 162; cf. Big. Bills and Notes, 82.

cause he who demanded payment did not have the bill with him.[1] For unless the paper were produced, how could the acceptor be able to judge its genuineness, the holder's right to receive payment, and immediately claim possession of it upon paying the amount? But if on demand the exhibition of the paper is not asked for, and payment declined on other grounds, the more formal presentment by actual exhibition of the paper is waived.[2]

§ 62. Where? Presentment for payment is made at the proper place: (1) Where a place of payment is specified in the instrument, and it is there presented; (2) Where no place of payment is specified, but the address of the person to make payment is given in the instrument and it is there presented; (3) Where no place of payment is specified, and no address is given, and the instrument is presented at the usual place of business or residence of the person to make payment; (4) In any other case, if presented to the person to make payment wherever he can be found, or if presented at his last known place of business or residence.[3]

ACCEPTANCE.

§ 63. Acceptance is the drawee's signification of his assent to the drawer's order. The Statute

[1] Freeman *v.* Boynton, 7 Mass. 483.

[2] Cf. Fall River Union Bank *v.* Willard, 5 Met. 216.

[3] R. L. ch. 73, § 90.

requires the acceptance to be in writing, and signed by the drawee; although by the law merchant an *oral* acceptance of an existing bill of exchange was valid, and an indorsee of a bill so accepted might maintain an action on such acceptance against the acceptor.[1] The customary method of accepting is for the drawee to write the word "accepted" across the face of the bill, and subscribe his name; but the acceptance may be on another paper, unless the holder making presentment for acceptance requires it to be written on the bill. If such request is refused, he may treat the bill as dishonored. And where an acceptance is written on a piece of paper other than the bill itself, it does not bind the acceptor except in favor of a person to whom it is shown, and who, on the faith thereof, receives the bill for value.[2]

§ 64. The drawee is allowed twenty-four hours after presentment in which to decide whether or not he will accept the bill; but the acceptance if given dates as of the day of presentation.[3] If not accepted within the prescribed time the person presenting it must treat the bill as dishonored or he loses the right of recourse against the drawer and

[1] Putnam Nat'l Bk. *v.* Snow, 172 Mass. 569. But this was simply because of the indorsee's right to elect to treat the oral promise as sufficient, and not because he was bound as indorsee to receive the oral acceptance in lieu of acceptance on the bill. Big. Bills and Notes, 53.

[2] R. L. ch. 73, §§ 149, 150, 151.

[3] R. L. ch. 73, § 153.

the indorsers.[1] But suppose that the drawee, instead of accepting the bill, destroys it; or refuses within twenty-four hours (or such time as the holder allows) after its delivery to return the bill, accepted or non-accepted, to the holder? He will be deemed to have accepted it.[2]

§ 65. A bill may be accepted while incomplete, when overdue, or after dishonor by a previous refusal to accept or by non-payment.[3] And an unconditional promise in writing to accept a bill before it is drawn is deemed an actual acceptance in favor of every person who, upon faith thereof, receives the bill for value.[4]

§ 66. The drawee of the bill of exchange himself, or his agent duly authorized, is the only one who can give an acceptance which will be binding. The acceptance by one partner of a bill drawn upon his firm suffices, for in that sense the partner is the agent of the firm.[5]

§ 67. The acceptance must not express that the drawee will perform his promise otherwise than by the payment of money.[6]

§ 68. An acceptance is either general or qualified. A general acceptance accepts without qualification to the order of the drawer. A qualified acceptance in express terms varies the effect of the bill as

[1] R. L. ch. 73, § 167.
[2] R. L. ch. 73, § 154.
[3] R. L. ch. 73, § 155.
[4] R. L. ch. 73, § 152. Cf. Exchange Bank *v.* Rice, 107 Mass. 37.
[5] Mason *v.* Rumsey, 1 Campb. 384.
[6] R. L. ch. 73, § 149.

drawn. An acceptance to pay at a particular place is a general acceptance unless it expressly states that the bill is to be paid there only and not elsewhere. An acceptance is qualified which is (1) conditional, that is to say, which makes payment by the acceptor dependent on the fulfilment of a condition therein stated; (2) partial, that is to say, an acceptance to pay part only of the amount for which the bill is drawn; (3) local, that is to say, an acceptance to pay only at a particular place; (4) qualified as to time; (5) the acceptance of some one or more of the drawees, but not of all. The holder may refuse (or instruct his notary to refuse) to take a qualified acceptance, and, if he does not obtain an unqualified acceptance, he may treat the bill as dishonored by non-acceptance. Where a qualified acceptance is taken the drawer and indorsers are discharged from liability on the bill, unless they have expressly or impliedly authorized the holder to take a qualified acceptance, or subsequently assented thereto. When the drawer or an indorser receives notice of a qualified acceptance, he must within a reasonable time express his dissent to the holder, or he will be deemed to have assented thereto.[1]

§ 69. A bill is dishonored by non-acceptance (1) if when duly presented for acceptance, such acceptance as the Statute requires is refused or cannot be obtained; or (2) where presentment

[1] R. L. ch. 73, §§ 156-159.

for acceptance is excused and the bill is not accepted.[1]

Payment.

§ 70. What is "payment"? Ordinarily the word "payment" is not a technical term.[2] Payment implies the existence of a debt, of a party to whom it is owed, and of a satisfaction of the debt to that party.[3] We have seen, however, that in the law of commercial paper, payment must be of a certain sum of money. But even the receipt of money is not always payment: thus, if money is received from a third person, not as payment of a note, but merely as security, the rights of the plaintiff against the defendant are not affected.[4]

2. NOTING.

§ 71. If acceptance or payment is refused, the notary should "note" the fact on the paper on the very day of dishonor.[5] The noting is a brief memorandum on the bill, or on a ticket attached to it, indicating the demand and protest for non-acceptance or non-payment, the date of dishonor, and the reasons therefor, if given, together with the notarial charges. This memorandum the notary

[1] R. L. ch. 73, § 166.

[2] 2 Greenl. Evid., 509.

[3] Tuttle v. Armstead, 53 Conn. 175.

[4] Commercial Natl. Bank v. Clark, 180 Mass. 249; Coleman v. Lewis (decided June 16, 1903, by Supreme Judicial Ct. of Mass.) not yet reported.

[5] Bailey v. Dozier, 6 How. 23; Cf. Leftley v. Mills, 4 T. R. 170.

ought to sign.[1] The noting is not the protest; but if the notary should die before making out the certificate, the noting may take its place, if it is intelligible, or can be so made. So if the certificate should be lost, or destroyed without the holder's consent.[2]

3. NOTICE OF DISHONOR.

§ 72. Except as the Statute otherwise provides, when a negotiable instrument has been dishonored by non-acceptance or non-payment, notice of dishonor must be given to the drawer and to each indorser, and any drawer or indorser to whom such notice is not given is discharged.[3]

(*a*) *Who may Give.*

§ 73. Notice of dishonor should be given (1) by the holder or by his authorized agent, usually a notary, and although by requirement of technical law it is no part of the notary's official duty in making protest to give notice of dishonor,[4] it is

[1] R. L. ch. 73, § 170; Smith *v.* Roach, 7 B. Monroe, 17.

[2] Big. Bills and Notes, 133.

[3] R. L. c. 73, § 106.

[4] Ins. Co. *v.* Wilson, 29 W. Va. 548; Burke *v.* McKay, 2 How. 66; Harris *v.* Robinson, 4 How. 336; Swayze *v.* Britton, 17 Kan. 625. "Indeed, a bank holding a bill or note for collection, or its officers or agents, should as a matter of duty give the notice necessary." Ogden *v.* Dobbin, 2 Hall. 112; Freeman's Bank *v.* Perkins, 7 Shep. 292; Bank of Mo. *v.* Vaughn, 36 Mo. 90. "But a notary

usual to the extent of custom in Massachusetts for him to do so; or (2) by an indorser legally bound to pay. It cannot be given, so as to have legal effect, by any other person; except, of course, on the death of the holder or the indorser, by his personal representative. This before, and probably since the Statute. The Statute declares that notice *may* be given by or on behalf of the holder, or by or on behalf of any party to the instrument who might be compelled to pay it to the holder, and who, upon taking it up, would have a right of reimbursement from the party to whom the notice is given. But "may" no doubt means "must," and "on behalf of," an authorized agent.[1] So of course notice by a stranger is insufficient.[2] It has been held that if the notice is sent by a notary to an indorser, and signed by mistake with the name of the maker as "notary public," it is invalid; for there is no such notary as he whose name is signed, and while the notice comes apparently from the maker of the note, it is not really from him, but is sent without his agency or authorized signa-

who presents and protests a bill of exchange is regarded, to a certain extent, as the agent of the holder, and is authorized, by his character and employment, to give notice to any of the other parties on the bill." Renick *v.* Robbins, 28 Mo. 339; Greene *v.* Farley, 20 Ala. 322. "The authority of the notary to demand payment of the bill and give the requisite notices is to be inferred from the fact that the bill was in his possession." Burbank *v.* Beach, 15 Barb. 326.

[1] Big. Bills and Notes, 142; R. L. ch. 73, §§ 107, 108.

[2] Lawrence *v.* Miller, 16 N. Y. 235.

ture;[1] and it has been further held that even a drawee who refuses acceptance cannot give notice.[2] The Statute declares that notice may be given by an agent either in his own name or in the name of any party entitled to give notice, whether that party is his principal or not.[3]

(*b*) *When Necessary?*

§ 74. Although by the general rule notice of dishonor must be given to the drawer and to each indorser, failing which the unnotified party is discharged, the Statute makes some important exceptions.

§ 75. Thus, notice of dishonor may be waived (*i. e.* the right thereto relinquished), either before the time of giving notice has arrived, or after the omission to give due notice. The waiver may be express or implied,[4] the latter and more unusual way being well illustrated by the following case. X., the maker of a promissory note not yet due, assigns all his property to Y., his indorser. Y. is to be considered as waiving demand and notice.[5]

§ 76. To constitute an express waiver, there should be an unqualified admission of liability, or

1 Cabot Bank *v.* Warner, 10 Allen, 522.
2 Stanton *v.* Blossom, 14 Mass. 116.
3 R. L. ch. 73, § 108.
4 R. L. ch. 73, § 126.
5 Tower *v.* Durell, 9 Mass. 332; Bond *v.* Farnham, 5 Mass. 170.

a direct promise to pay.[1] Hence the indorser's words, "The note will be paid," do not constitute a waiver of notice. Equivocal language cannot constitute a waiver. But the waiver may be oral.[2] If embodied in the instrument, the waiver binds all parties; but where it is written above an indorser's signature, it binds him only.[3]

§ 77. A waiver of protest, whether in the case of a foreign bill or other negotiable instrument, is deemed to be a waiver not only of a formal protest, but also of presentment and notice of dishonor.[4]

§ 78. Notice of dishonor is dispensed with when, after the exercise of reasonable diligence, it cannot be given or does not reach the parties sought to be charged. What is "reasonable diligence" is, ordinarily, according to Chalmers, a question of fact;[5] and according to Benjamin, a mixed question of law and fact.[6] Thus, if the holder of a dishonored bill does not know the indorser's address, and makes some inquiry, but does not take the steps he reasonably might have done, the indorser is discharged.[7] But "when the facts are all ascertained, what is reasonable diligence is a question of

[1] Glidden *v.* Chamberlin, 167 Mass. 486.

[2] Creamer *v.* Perry, 17 Pick. 332.

[3] R. L. ch. 73, § 127.

[4] R. L. ch. 73, § 128.

[5] Chalmers, Bills of Exchange (5th Ed. English), 165.

[6] Benjamin's Chalmers, 201.

[7] Beveridge *v.* Burgess, 3 Campb. 262.

law."[1] "This results from the necessity of having some fixed legal standard, by which men may not only know the law but be protected by it."[2]

§ 79. Notice of dishonor is not required to be given to the drawer (1) where the drawer and drawee are the same person; (2) where the drawee is a fictitious person or has not capacity to contract; (3) where the drawer is the person to whom the instrument is presented for payment; (4) where the drawer has no right to expect or require that the drawee or acceptor will honor the instrument, or where the drawer has countermanded payment. Notice to an indorser is not required (1) where the drawee is a fictitious person, or has not capacity to contract, and the indorser was aware of the fact when he indorsed the instrument; (2) where the indorser is the person to whom the instrument is presented for payment; (3) where the instrument was made or accepted for his accommodation.[3]

§ 80. Where due notice of dishonor by non-acceptance has been given, notice of a subsequent dishonor by non-payment is not necessary, unless meanwhile the instrument has been accepted. An omission to give notice of dishonor by non-acceptance does not prejudice the rights of a holder in due course after the omission.[4]

[1] Bank of Utica *v.* Bender, 21 Wend. 643.

[2] Bryden *v.* Bryden, 11 Johns. 187.

[3] R. L. ch. 73, §§ 131, 132.

[4] R. L. ch. 73, §§ 133, 134.

§ 81. Where any negotiable instrument has been dishonored, it may be protested for non-acceptance or non-payment, as the case may be; but protest is not required, except in the case of foreign bills of exchange.[1]

(c) *Form of Notice.*

§ 82. The notice may be in writing or merely oral, and may be given in any terms which sufficiently identify the instrument and indicate that it has been dishonored by non-acceptance or non-payment.[2] Thus, a notice to the indorser was held good which simply stated that the note (which was described) was protested for non-payment, and that the holders looked to the person to whom the notice was sent for payment. This even before the Statute.[3]

§ 83. A written notice need not be signed, and an insufficient written notice may be supplemented and validated by verbal communication. Nor does a misdescription of the instrument vitiate the notice unless the party to whom the notice is given is in fact misled thereby.[4] For example, a notice to

[1] R. L. ch. 73, § 135.

[2] R. L. ch. 73, § 113.

[3] Legg *v.* Vinal, 165 Mass. 155; Housatonic Bank *v.* Laflin, 5 Cush. 546. The notice in the latter case ran thus: "New York, Dec. 16, 1848. Mr. Cutter Laflin. Sir, Please to take notice that a promissory note drawn by P. D. Whitney, agent, for $750, indorsed by you, is protested for non-payment thereof. Your obedient servant, A. R. Rodgers, notary public."

[4] R. L. ch. 73, § 112.

an indorser, seasonably given, suffices, although, without leading the indorser astray, it misstates the maturity of the note and the maker's name.[1]

§ 84. So a notice by a notary is sufficient which does not state who owns the note, or at whose request the notice is given.[2]

§ 85. So if the maker of a note has left the Commonwealth before the maturity of the note, the notice to the indorser of non-payment need not state this fact. Enough if the demand for payment has been left at the last and usual place of abode of the maker, or at his place of business.[3]

§ 86. But before and probably since the Statute a notice to the holder of a note, which merely states that the note remains unpaid, and that the holders look to him for payment, is not sufficient to charge the indorser, although the notice be given by a notary public. The notice must be such as to assert or imply that the note has been presented and payment refused, or has been otherwise dishonored.[4]

§ 87. Neither the Statute nor the law merchant prescribes any particular words for giving notice of dishonor. The following form is suggested.

[1] Smith *v.* Whiting, 12 Mass. 6.

[2] Shed *v.* Brett, 1 Pick. 401.

[3] Sanger *v.* Stimpson, 8 Mass. 260.

[4] Pinkham *v.* Macy, 9 Met. 174.

Form.

B........................,.............., 190 .

M..

You are notified that a [bill of exchange, promissory note or check] for.......................................dollars $\frac{}{100}$, dated........................,........................, [drawn or indorsed by you], has been [protested or noted] by me for non- [payment or acceptance] after due presentment and demand made upon the [maker or drawee] this day, and that you are held answerable for the amount, with all legal costs, interests and damages in consequence of the non-[payment or acceptance] thereof.

R. B., *Notary Public.*

(*d*) *When to be Made and Given.*

§ 88. Notice may be given as soon as the instrument is dishonored; and unless delay is excused as the Statute provides, *must* be given within the times fixed by the Statute.[1]

§ 89. Where the person giving and the person to receive notice reside in the *same* place, the Statute declares that notice must be given within the following times: (1) If given at the place of business of the person to receive notice, it must be given before the close of business hours on the day following; (2) if given at his residence, it

[1] R. L. ch. 73, § 119.

must be given before the usual hours of rest on the day following; (3) if sent by mail, it must be deposited in the post-office in time to reach him in usual course on the day following.[1]

§ 90. But where the person giving and the person to receive notice reside in *different* places, the notice must be given within the following times: (1) If sent by mail, it must be deposited in the post-office in time to go by mail the day following the day of dishonor, or if there is no mail at a convenient hour on that day, by the next mail thereafter.[2] It is the holder's duty to use due diligence in ascertaining the hour at which the mail closes on the day following the day of dishonor, and to put his notices into the office seasonably to go forward by that mail. His failure to do so is such laches as to render the notices insufficient to charge the indorsers. Ten o'clock in the morning is a "convenient hour."[3] (2) If notice is given otherwise than through the post-office, then within the time that the notice would have been received in due course of mail if it had been deposited in the post-office within the time specified in (1).

§ 91. When is delay in giving notice of dishonor excused? When the delay is caused by circumstances beyond the holder's control, and not imputable to his default, misconduct or negli-

[1] R. L. ch. 73, § 120.

[2] R. L. ch. 73, § 121.

[3] Haskell *v.* Boardman, 8 Allen, 38.

gence.[1] Thus, by the custom of Cuba in former years, very little business was done from December 25 to January 6, the Christmas holidays. Vessels were not allowed to clear from port; hence it was unnecessary during this period to write a notice of dishonor to be sent to a foreign port.[2] In a curious English case Lord Ellenborough held a Jewish festival to be ground for delay.[3] But when the cause of delay ceases to operate, notice must be given with reasonable diligence.[4]

§ 92. To sum up the Statute, notice may be given either on the day of the dishonor, being the day of maturity, or on the first following secular day; and it must be given on one of these days, unless the delay is excused. And there is "no case in which, by the law merchant, notice must be given on the day of dishonor, however easily it might be done, and whatever the consequences of not doing it."[5]

§ 93. Where a party receives notice of dishonor, he has, after the receipt of such notice, the same time for giving notice to antecedent parties that the holder has after the dishonor.[6]

[1] R. L. ch. 73, § 130.
[2] Martin *v.* Ingersoll, 8 Pick. 1.
[3] Lindo *v.* Unsworth, 2 Camp. 602; 12 Rev. Rep. 750.
[4] R. L. ch. 73, § 130.
[5] Big. Bills and Notes, 151.
[6] R. L. ch. 73, § 124.

(e) *How and Where to be Given.*

How?

§ 94. The law merchant requires that the indorser shall be notified of the dishonor of commercial paper with reasonable despatch, and the Statute appears to treat notice by mail in all cases as consistent with that requirement, for it declares that where notice is duly addressed and deposited in the post-office, the sender is deemed to have given due notice, notwithstanding any miscarriage in the mails.[1] Notice is deemed to have been deposited in the post-office when deposited in any branch post-office or in any letter-box under the control of the post-office department.[2]

§ 95. Prior to the passage of Acts of 1871, chapter 239, the holder of a bill or note could not give notice of its dishonor through the mail to an indorser or drawer who lived in the same city or town, but must give the notice to him personally, or at his place of business or residence. The chief object of that Act was to extend the privilege of giving notice by mail to cases where the parties live

[1] R. L. ch. 73, § 122; Wamesit Bank *v.* Buttrick, 11 Gray, 387; Lamkin *v.* Edgerly, 151 Mass. 348. In the former case, Bigelow, J., said, "The notices having been seasonably and properly put into the post-office, it is immaterial that they were never received and forwarded by reason of being lost in the mail. Due diligence did not require anything further to be done in order to hold the indorsers."

[2] R. L. ch. 73, § 123.

in the same place.[1] But if it is desirable, the notice may be served by messenger at the residence or place of business of the indorser or drawer.[2]

§ 96. Under the provisions stated in Revised Laws, chapter 73, § 122, a notice to an indorser of a promissory note of its non-payment, duly deposited, postage prepaid, in the post-office in the town in which he lives, the direction on the envelope in which it is enclosed containing only his name and that of the town, is sufficient, although he lives on a street which has a name, if the houses on the street are not numbered, and there is no postal delivery by carriers; and the facts that he did not receive the notice, and that another person of the same name lived in the town who did not receive it, are immaterial.[3]

§ 97. Where the notice is served at an indorser's office, it must be served during business hours, unless some one is there to receive it;[4] but where it is served at his residence, it may be served at any reasonable hour before bedtime.[5]

§ 98. Where the indorser of a promissory note resides in a town where there are two post-offices, of which fact the holder of the note is ignorant, a notice of the dishonor of the note, addressed to the indorser at the town generally, is sufficient, unless

1 Wachusett National Bank *v.* Fairbrother, 148 Mass. 181.

2 Story, Prom. Notes, § 340; Big. Bills and Notes, 150.

3 Morse *v.* Chamberlin, 144 Mass. 406.

4 Bonner *v.* New Orleans, 2 Woods (U. S.), 135.

5 2 Edwards, Notes and Bills, § 829.

he proves that he is accustomed to receive his letters at one of the offices only, and that the holder of the note might have ascertained that fact by reasonable inquiry.[1]

§ 99. A notice sent by mail to an indorser and addressed with the name of the town or city alone, no street and number being used, is sufficient to charge the indorser, if he in fact lives in the town or city named, and unless it appears that there was another person of the same name in the same place.[2]

§ 100. A notice of the non-payment of a note, addressed and sent in due season by mail to an indorser at the post-office where he usually receives his letters, and received by him there on the day after the note fell due, is sufficient to fix his liability thereon, although such post-office is in another part of the same town.[3]

§ 101. An indorser who lives in a town where there is a post-office, is not properly notified of the dishonor of an instrument by a drop-letter left for him in the post-office of another town where the holder resides, and addressed to the indorser as if he also resided there, even though it appears that the indorser is in the habit of resorting to the post-office in each of the two places.[4]

§ 102. Sending notice to the indorser according

[1] Burlingame *v.* Foster, 128 Mass. 125.

[2] True *v.* Collins, 3 Allen, 438.

[3] Shaylor *v.* Mix, 4 Allen, 351.

[4] Shelburne Falls Bank *v.* Townsley, 107 Mass. 444.

to an established usage is sufficient, whether the indorser receives it or not.[1] Thus, a notice of the non-payment of a promissory note, addressed to the indorser and deposited in a post-office box in a public street, is sufficient, that being the customary way of sending letters;[2] and for the same reason notices of non-payment of a promissory note addressed to all the indorsers respectively, and enclosed in a letter to the last indorser, are sufficient to charge the prior indorsers.[3]

§ 103. Where a notary seasonably left a notice of non-payment at a shop near the indorser's place of business, because the indorser was out of town, it was said to be extremely doubtful whether this was sufficient, although the indorser took away the notice the next day or the day after. "Although a man is out of town, yet if he has a domicile or place of business, it is to be presumed that he will leave some person charged with the care of his business, or at least some one between whom and himself there is a privity or confidence. It is upon this principle that all notices at one's domicile, and all notices respecting transactions of a commercial nature at one's known place of business, are deemed in law to be good constructive notice, and to have the legal effect of actual notice."[4]

[1] Lincoln & Kennebec Bank v. Hammatt, 9 Mass. 159.

[2] Johnson v. Brown, 154 Mass. 105.

[3] Wamesit Bank v. Buttrick, 11 Gray, 387.

[4] Shaw, C. J., in Granite Bank v. Ayers, 16 Pick. 392.

§ 104. Where a promissory note specifies no place of payment, a presentment of it at the former place of business of the maker, without any inquiry as to his place of residence, is not a good presentment to charge an indorser. The presentment at the former place of business, without any inquiry as to the place of residence, does not show such diligent search for the maker and failure to find him as would excuse a want of presentment of the note and demand of payment.[1]

§ 105. Thus it may be seen that "residence" in the law of negotiable instruments is not used in a strict sense as necessarily implying a permanent, exclusive or actual abode in the place, but it may be satisfied by a temporary, partial or even constructive residence.[2]

Where?

§ 106. Where a party has added an address to his signature, notice of dishonor must be sent to that address; but if he has not given such address, then the notice must be sent as follows: (1) Either to the post-office nearest to his place of residence, or to the post-office where he is accustomed to receive his letters;[3] or it seems, where these facts are not known to the notifying party, to the town

---

[1] Talbot *v.* National Bank of the Commonwealth, 129 Mass. 67.

[2] Wachusett National Bank *v.* Fairbrother, 148 Mass. 181.

[3] R. L. ch. 73, § 125.

without naming any particular post-office.[1] And if the indorser lives in a very sparsely settled part of the state, and there is no post-office in the town in which he lives, the holder does his duty if he sends notice directed to the indorser at the nearest town having a post-office, so far as can be ascertained by reasonable inquiry.[2] (2) If he lives in one place, and has his place of business in another, notice may be sent to either place: or (3) if he is sojourning in another place, notice may be sent to the place where he is so sojourning.[3] But where the notice is actually received by the party within the time specified in the Statute, it will be sufficient, though not sent in accordance with the requirements of section 125 of the Statute as above stated. Thus, notice may be given to the indorser personally, anywhere, wherever the holder or notifying indorser may happen to find him, so far as place is concerned; it may be given to him in his house or counting-room, in the cars, or on the street, so long as it is good in other respects. This is because the notice is a mere warning, and not expected to be followed by payment on the spot, as is presentment for payment.[4] But notice in some form he must have; mere knowledge of the dishonor is not enough.[5]

1 Big. Bills and Notes, 158.

2 Big. Bills and Notes, 160; Shed *v.* Brett, 1 Pick. 401.

3 R. L. ch. 73, § 125.

4 Big. Bills and Notes, 158; Hyslop *v.* Jones, 3 McLean, 96.

5 Big. Bills and Notes, 133, 134.

(*f*) *To Whom to be Given.*

§ 107. We have already seen that except as the Statute otherwise provides, when a negotiable instrument has been dishonored by non-acceptance or non-payment, notice of dishonor must be given to the drawer and to each indorser, and that any drawer or indorser to whom such notice is not given is discharged. And a person becoming a party to a non-negotiable promissory note payable on time, by a signature in blank (*i. e.* by a signature which does not mention the name of the person in whose favor it is made) is entitled to notice of non-payment the same as an indorser.

§ 108. Notice of dishonor may be given either to the party himself (*i. e.* the indorser) or to his authorized agent.[1] Where the parties to be notified are partners, notice to one is notice to the firm, even though there has been a dissolution.[2] And although after the partnership had been dissolved, and all of the partners have gone away, if a notice of the dishonor is given at the place where they formerly did business, and is received by an agent appointed to wind up the partnership, the notice is sufficient, if the holder did not know of the dissolution.[3] But if two or more not partners have indorsed the paper jointly, notice must be given to

[1] R. L. ch. 73, § 114.
[2] R. L. ch. 73, § 116.
[3] Bliss *v.* Nichols, 12 Allen, 443.

each of them (if by due diligence it can be done); unless one of them has authority to receive such notice for the others.[1]

§ 109. But suppose the party to be notified is dead, to the knowledge of the holder? Who shall be notified? If there be a personal representative of the deceased (*i. e.* an executor, whether he has qualified or not, or an administrator already appointed), notice should be given to such person, provided he can be found with reasonable diligence.[2] If there are two or more, notice to one is notice to all. If there is no personal representative of the deceased indorser, still the holder should use reasonable diligence to inform those interested in his estate of the dishonor of the paper. Hence if notice is sent to the last place of residence or of business of the indorser, that is enough, *prima facie*, to fix the liability of his estate. Common sense would tell that generally the notice would reach those chiefly interested.[3] When notice is sent to the personal representative, it should be addressed to him by name if this can be learned by reasonable diligence: — thus, "to John Smith," not "to the executor of Charles Childes," the deceased indorser, though notice so addressed is good if received in due time.[4]

[1] R. L. ch. 73, § 117.
[2] R. L. ch. 73, § 115.
[3] Dodson *v.* Taylor, 56 N. J. 11; Big. Bills and Notes, 145.
[4] Big. Bills and Notes, 146.

§ 110. Where a party has been adjudged a bankrupt or an insolvent, or has made an assignment for the benefit of creditors, notice of dishonor may be given either to the party himself or to his trustee or assignee.[1]

4. EXTENDING THE PROTEST.

§ 111. While the notary must "note" the fact of the dishonor of an instrument to be protested on the very day of its dishonor, unless the Statute excuses his delay, the protest may be made out in full at any subsequent time down to the time of suit on the paper. The act of making the complete, formal protest is called "extending the protest," and this may be done as of the date of the noting.[2]

§ 112. The protest must be annexed to the bill (or other paper) or must contain a copy thereof, must be under the hand and seal of the notary making it, and must specify, (1) the time and place of presentment, (2) the fact and manner thereof, (3) the cause or reason of protest, and (4) the demand made and answer given, if any, or the fact that the drawee or acceptor could not be found.[3]

[1] R. L. ch. 73, § 118.

[2] R. L. ch. 73, § 172; Big. Bills and Notes, 133.

[3] R. L. ch. 73, § 170.

FORMS.

No. 1. *Protest of a Bill for Non-acceptance.*

COMMONWEALTH OF MASSACHUSETTS.

[Name of County] } ss.

On the day of , in the year of our Lord one thousand nine hundred and , I, R. B., Notary Public, duly admitted and sworn, and practising in said county, and in the city [*or* town] of B. at the request of C. D. of B. aforesaid, [*or* of "the holder" *or* "the bearer," *as the case may be*] went with the original bill of exchange [*or* "did exhibit the original bill of exchange"] which is hereto annexed, [*or* "whereof a true copy is on the other side written"], the time therein limited having fully elapsed, to [*or* at the counting-house of] E. F., the person upon whom the said bill is drawn, and demanded acceptance of the said bill of him in person, [*or* of G. H., a clerk of the said E. F., authorized to accept or refuse acceptance on his behalf] and received for answer that it would not be accepted at present [*or whatever other answer was given*].

The bill remaining unaccepted, I duly and officially notified the drawer and indorsers [*here state manner of sending notice, e. g.* by mailing notice properly addressed to them (postage prepaid)] of said non-acceptance.

Wherefore I, the said Notary, by request as aforesaid, have protested and by these presents do solemnly protest against the drawer of said bill and all others concerned therein, for exchange, re-exchange, and all costs, charges, damages, and interest, suffered and sustained, or to be suffered and sustained, by reason or in consequence of the non-acceptance thereof.

{SEAL.} In testimony whereof, I have hereunto set my hand and affixed my notarial seal, the day and year first above written.

FEES. { }

$——

R. B., *Notary Public.*

No. 2. *Protest of a Bill for Non-acceptance when the Drawee cannot be found, or when there is no such Person.*

[*Begin as in Form* 1 *above, for* "*Protest of a Bill for Non-acceptance.*"]

On the day of , [*following Form* 1] did make and cause to be made due and careful inquiries at , and in other proper quarters, for E. F., the person upon whom the said bill purports to be drawn, in order to have demanded acceptance thereof, but was unable to discover him, or to learn any tidings of him or of his residence. [*Here state sending of notice of dishonor, as in Form* 1.]

Wherefore, I, the said Notary [*conclude as in Form* 1].

In testimony whereof, etc.

{SEAL} R. B., *Notary Public.*

No. 3. *Protest of a Bill, by a Resident Person in a Place where there is no Notary.*[1]

COMMONWEALTH OF MASSACHUSETTS.

[Name of County] } ss.

On the day of , one thousand nine hundred and , I, A. B., a substantial person, residing at B. in the county of , and in the Commonwealth aforesaid, at the request of the holder of a certain bill of exchange hereto annexed [*or* whereof a true copy is on the other side written], did exhibit the said original bill of exchange unto Mr. of B., aforesaid, the person upon whom the same is drawn, and demanded acceptance thereof, who answered that [*here state his answer and refusal*] and I, the said A. B., do hereby certify that there is no public notary practising in or near B. , afore-

[1] We have seen elsewhere that under the Statute, R. L. ch. 73, § 171, "protest may be made (1) by a notary public, or (2) by any respectable resident of the place when the bill is dishonored, in the presence of two or more credible witnesses." Dr. Bigelow interprets the Statute as giving no preference to the notary's act, and changing the unwritten law, which imputes no notarial force to a protest by a private citizen, unless he acts when no notary can be found to serve. The above form is in conformity with the law merchant; it may be changed to meet the needs of a private person who sees fit to protest paper, when a notary is at hand and obtainable, by omitting the following quoted words: "And I, the said A. B., do hereby certify that there is no public notary practising in or near B , aforesaid;" . . . "and in the absence of and in default of a public notary at this place." See Big. Bills and Notes (as to the interpretation of the Statute), 125. The matter has not been decided by the courts; and such protest is certainly not custom and would be unsafe.

said. Wherefore I, the said, A. B., at the request aforesaid, and in the absence of and in default of a public notary at this place, have protested, and by these presents do protest against the drawer of the said bill, and all other parties thereto, and all others concerned, for all exchange, re-exchange, and all costs, damages, and interest, present and to come, for want of acceptance thereof, in the presence of C. D. and E. F., both credible persons residing at B. aforesaid.

Which I attest,

A. B.,

a housekeeper and merchant [*or* a manufacturer, or an attorney-at-law, *or* banker, *or* hotel-keeper, &c., &c.], residing at B. , aforesaid.[1]

G. H. }
J. K. } *Witnesses.*

No. 4. *Shorter Form of Protest of a Bill by a Resident Person in a Place where there is no Notary.*

Know all men that I, A. B. [merchant, *or* banker, *etc.*, *as the case may be*] of in the County of and Commonwealth of Massachusetts, at

[1] For form, see Brooke's Notary, 295 [2d ed.], which declares that by the law merchant it does not appear to be necessary that there should be witnesses to the protest of a foreign bill by a private citizen. *Contra*, Todd *v.* M'Neal's Admr., 49 Ala. 273. Cf. Daniel & Douglass, Elements of Neg. Instr., 227. Chitty on Bills, *333 [374] n. *u*. And witnesses are required by the Statute.

the request of C.D., there being no notary public available, did on the day of , 190 , at , demand payment [*or* acceptance] of the bill of exchange hereunder written, from E. F., to which demand he made answer [*state answer, if any*], wherefore I now, in the presence of G. H. and J. K., do protest the said bill of exchange.

(Signed) A. B.

G. H. }
J. K. } *Witnesses.*

[The bill itself should be annexed, or a copy of the bill and all that is written thereon should be underwritten.[1]]

No. 5. *Protest of a Bill for Non-payment.*

COMMONWEALTH OF MASSACHUSETTS.

[Name of County.] } ss.

On the day of , in the year of our Lord one thousand nine hundred and , I, R. B., Notary Public, duly admitted and sworn, and practising in said County and in the city [*or* town] of B. at the request of C. D. of B. aforesaid [*or* of "the holder" *or* "the bearer," *as the case may be*] went with the original bill of exchange, [*or* "did exhibit the original bill of exchange"] which is hereto annexed, [*or* "a true copy whereof is on the other side written"] the time therein limited having fully elapsed, unto E. F., the

[1] For form, see Brooke's Notary, 173 [6th ed.]

person upon whom the said bill is drawn, and by whom the same is accepted, [*if the bill has been accepted,*] [*or, as the case may be,* unto a clerk in the counting-house of the said E. F., he being absent or inaccessible] and demanded payment thereof, [*or* payment being thereupon demanded,] and he answered that it would not be paid.

The bill remaining unpaid, I duly and officially notified the drawer and indorsers [*here state manner of sending notice, e. g.* by mailing notices properly addressed to them (postage prepaid)] of said non-payment, requiring payment.

Wherefore I, the said Notary, by request as aforesaid, have protested and by these presents do solemnly protest, against the drawer of said bill and all others concerned therein, for exchange, re-exchange, and all costs, charges, damages, and interest, suffered and sustained, or to be suffered and sustained, by reason or in consequence of the non-payment thereof.

{SEAL.} In testimony whereof, I have hereunto set my hand and affixed my notarial seal, the day and year first above written.

FEES.
- Noting non-acceptance . .
- Postage . . . .
- Protesting for non-payment
- Postage . . . . .

$——

R. B., *Notary Public.*

[The above form may easily be altered to meet the case of a check.]

No. 6. *Protest of a Promissory Note.*

[Here affix the original note or a copy.]

COMMONWEALTH OF MASSACHUSETTS.

[Name of County] } ss.

On this day of , in the year of our Lord one thousand nine hundred and , I, A. B., Notary Public by legal authority, duly admitted and sworn, and practising in said county, and in the town [*or* city] of B., at the request of [the holder], of , went with the original note [*if a copy instead is annexed so state*], which is hereto annexed, the time limited therein having elapsed, to [the maker, *or* place of payment] and demanded payment [*here state manner of demanding payment*].

The note remaining unpaid, I have officially notified the [*e. g.* first, second and third] indorsers of the said default by notice addressed to them, and [*here state method of notification*].

Wherefore I, the said Notary, at the request aforesaid, have protested, and by these presents do solemnly protest against the maker of said note, the indorsers, and all others whom it doth or may concern, for exchange, re-exchange, and all costs, charges, damages and interest, suffered, sustained and incurred, or to be suffered, sustained and incurred by reason or in consequence of the non-payment of said note.

{ SEAL. } Thus done and protested in [town or city] aforesaid, and my notarial seal affixed, the day and year first above written.

A. B., *Notary Public.*

CHARGES :

Noting,
Protest,
Record,
Notice,
Postage,

$

LIABILITY OF NOTARIES.

(*a*) *Negligence.*

§ 113. A notary who fails to make a protest when it is required, or who neglects to give proper notice to parties to be charged in case of dishonor, will be liable for the loss occasioned by his neglect; but since the notary is one in whom confidence is reposed by the very nature of the office which he holds, a charge of negligence against him in making presentment and demand, or in giving notice of dishonor, can only be established by full and satisfactory proof of the matters alleged. "The fact of negligence must not only be proved, but the further fact, that the plaintiffs thereby sustained damage. . . . Actual loss sustained is the cause of action."[1]

[1] Shaw, C. J., in Warren Bank *v.* Parker, 8 Gray, 221.

(*b*) *Standard of Diligence.*

§ 114. A notary is required to exercise due diligence in the discharge of his duties as regards commercial paper, but the law does not require of the holder of a negotiable instrument, or of his agent the notary public, the highest and strictest degree of diligence in giving notice of its dishonor, but only such a degree of reasonable diligence as will ordinarily bring notice home to the party; and less diligence is required in ascertaining the residence for the purpose of giving notice than for the purpose of making a demand of payment.[1] Thus notice of the dishonor of a bill or note is sufficient to charge an indorser or drawer if it is delivered to him personally, or is left at his place of residence or of business, the postage being prepaid.[2] Going to the place of business of the maker of a note, in business hours, with the note, to demand payment of it and finding it shut, without any person to answer inquiries, is using due diligence, and excuses a want of demand, although the note is not expressly payable at such place of business.[3] Where the holder of a bill drawn by a person who had been absent from the state for several years left a notice at his last dwelling-house, none of his

1 Wachusett National Bank *v.* Fairbrother, 148 Mass. 181; Hobbs *v.* Straine, 149 Mass. 212.

2 Bank of America *v.* Shaw, 142 Mass. 290; Importers and Traders' Bank *v.* Shaw, 144 Mass. 421.

3 Shed *v.* Brett, 1 Pick. 413.

family residing there, which came to the hands of the drawer's wife, it was thought that due diligence had been used.[1]

§ 115. But where a note was dated at Boston, where the maker and all the indorsers resided, it was held that the fact that the notary's protest recited that he went to various places in Boston, making diligent inquiry of different people for the promisor, but could not find him, nor any one knowing him, nor any one with the funds for the payment of the note, and thereupon sent notices to the several indorsers, did not show reasonable diligence to find the maker which would excuse a want of a presentment and demand, it appearing otherwise that the notary knew where to find the indorsers and neglected to make inquiries of them for the maker.[2] And where the holder of a note of a firm presented it at the last place of business of the makers, which was then occupied by strangers, and was told that the makers had gone out of the city without leaving any funds, whereupon he made no further inquiry for them, but in fact one of them lived in the city and his name and place of residence were in the directory, it was held that there had not been sufficient diligence to excuse a demand.[3]

[1] Blakely *v.* Grant, 6 Mass. 386.

[2] Porter *v.* Judson, 1 Gray, 175.

[3] Granite Bank *v.* Ayers, 16 Pick. 392.

SELECTION OF A NOTARY BY A BANK.

§ 116. While it is unquestionably true that a bank receiving a promissory note for collection is bound to use due care and diligence in demanding payment of the maker, and giving notice of the non-payment, it is equally true that where the nature of the business in which an agent, for example, a bank, is engaged requires for its proper and reasonable execution the employment of a sub-agent, for example, a notary, the principal agent is not responsible for the acts of the sub-agent, provided a proper sub-agent was selected.

§ 117. Thus, in an action against a bank for negligence in not duly demanding payment of a note left with them for collection, the defence being that the note was duly placed in the hands of a competent notary public for demand and protest, and that the negligence, if any, was on his part (the defendants having been the collecting agents for the plaintiffs for more than ten years, and having invariably placed their notes in the hands of a notary for demand and protest, with the knowledge of the plaintiffs), evidence is admissible for the defendants of an invariable usage among Boston banks, among them the defendants, when notes are sent to them for collection, to keep the same for payment until the close of banking hours, and if not then paid, to put them in the hands of a notary for demand and protest, and that the defendants did so in the present case; and it was held that if these facts be established, the defendant bank is not responsible for the notary's negligence.[1]

BANK OFFICERS.

§ 118. What are the rights of notaries public who are bank officers, touching the protest of the bank's commercial paper? A notary who is an officer of a bank may legally protest paper belonging to the bank,[2] even though he is also a stockholder.[3] And it has been held that the cashier of a bank, who is a notary, may legally protest his own note which has been discounted by the bank.[4]

RECORDS.

§ 119. Proffat says, "In a large majority of our states," including Massachusetts, "notaries are required to keep a register, in which they shall record their official acts, and especially their acts in relation to the notice and protest regarding negotiable paper; to keep a correct record of such

1 Warren Bank *v.* Suffolk Bank, 10 Cush. 582 [1852].

2 Nelson *v.* First Nat'l Bk., 69 Fed. R. 798.

3 Moreland's Assignee *v.* Citizens' Savings Bk. (Ky.), 30 S. W. Rep. 19.

4 Dykman *v.* Northbridge, 1 App. Div. (N. Y.) 26; Crawford, Neg. Inst. Law, 130.

protest, the time and manner served, and names of all parties to whom notice is directed, and description and amount of the instrument protested, which record is [in certain cases] competent to prove such notice in any court where proof is required, and such record is required to be open to public inspection, and in a few of the states the law requires notaries to record a copy of every certificate of protest and promissory note or other negotiable instrument. There are strict rules and provisions in regard to this duty in the statutes."[1]

§ 120. In Massachusetts, upon the death, resignation or removal from office of a notary public, his records and official papers shall be deposited in the office of the clerk of the courts in the county in which he resided, or, if he resided in the county of Suffolk, in the office of the clerk of the superior court of said county for civil business. Said clerks must safely keep such records and official papers, and shall make and certify copies thereof.[2]

§ 121. A notary public who neglects for three months after his resignation or removal from office so to deposit his records and official papers, or the executor or administrator of a deceased notary public who neglects for three months after his acceptance of such office so to deposit such records and official papers of the deceased which come into his hands, shall forfeit not more than five hundred

[1] Proffat, Notaries, § 30 [2d ed.].

[2] R. L. ch. 17, § 2.

dollars.[1] And whoever knowingly destroys, defaces or conceals the records or official papers of a notary public, shall forfeit not more than one thousand dollars and be liable for damages to any person injured thereby.[2]

PROTEST FOR BETTER SECURITY.

§ 122. Besides the protest for non-acceptance and for non-payment, the holder may protest a bill for better security. Protest for better security is where the acceptor has been adjudged a bankrupt or an insolvent, or has made an assignment for the benefit of creditors.[3] In such case, the holder may cause a notary to demand better security,[4] and, on its being refused, may cause the bill to be protested for better security against the drawer and indorsers,[5] and notice of the protest to be sent to them. Yet, it seems, the holder must wait till the bill falls due before he can sue any party. Nor does there appear any advantage from the protest more than from simple notice of the circumstances, except that, after such a protest, there may be a second acceptance for honor; whereas, without the intervention of a protest, there cannot be two acceptances on the same bill.

[1] R. L. ch. 17, § 3.
[2] R. L. ch. 17, § 4.
A suitable record book may be obtained at any law-stationer's.
[3] R. L. ch. 73, § 175. [4] Byles on Bills, 263.
[5] R. L. ch. 73, § 175.

§ 122 *a*. The following case quaintly but clearly illustrates the meaning of the phrase "protest for better security" albeit the great judge who decided the case belongs to an era remote in the history of commercial paper in England.

Per Holt, C. J. "The custom of merchants is, that if B., upon whom a bill of exchange is drawn, absconds before the day of payment, the man to whom it is payable may protest it, to have better security for the payment, and to give notice to the drawer of the absconding of B., and after time of payment is incurred, then it ought to be protested for non-payment the same day of payment or after it. But no protest for non-payment can be before the day that it is payable. Proved by merchants at *Guildhall*, *Trin.* 6 *W. & M.* before *Treby*, chief justice. And the plaintiff was non-suit, because he had declared, upon a custom, to protest for non-payment before the day of payment."[1]

§ 122 *b*. And in conclusion, query if there *is* any custom of protest for better security in Massachusetts, apart from the Statute?

Form of Protest of a Bill for Better Security.

COMMONWEALTH OF MASSACHUSETTS.

[Name of County] } ss.

On the day of , one thousand nine hundred and , I, R. B., Notary Public, duly admitted and

[1] *Ex relatione* Place, Anon. 1 Ld. Raym. 743.

sworn, and practising in said county, and at the request of C. D. of B. in the county of aforesaid, [*or* of the holder, *or* the bearer] did exhibit the original bill of exchange which is hereto annexed, [*or* whereof a true copy is on the other side written,] at the counting-house of E. F., the person upon whom the said bill is drawn, and whose acceptance appears thereon, and did present the same unto a clerk there, and demand better security for the payment thereof when the same should become payable, in consequence of the said E. F. having become bankrupt, [*or* insolvent, *or* made an assignment for the benefit of creditors,] and I received for answer, that security for the same could not be given by the said E. F., who had become bankrupt [*or* insolvent, *or* had assigned for the benefit of creditors, *as the case may be*].

Wherefore I, the said notary, at the request aforesaid, have protested, and by these presents do protest against the drawer of the said bill, and the acceptor and all other parties thereto, and all parties concerned, for all exchange, re-exchange, and all costs, damages, and interest, present and to come, for want of better security, for the payment of the said bill when due.

{SEAL.} Which I attest,

R. B.,
Notary Public.

ACCEPTANCE FOR HONOR.

§ 123. Acceptance for honor, sometimes called acceptance *supra protest*, because it always follows protest, if received at all, is not in use in this country to the extent of custom,[1] although discussed and admitted in an early Massachusetts case;[2] but the Statute in Massachusetts provides for it as if it were in frequent use here, adopting the law of England, where the law is only an expression of actual custom.[3]

§ 124. When a bill of exchange has been protested for dishonor by non-acceptance, or protested for better security and is not overdue, any person not being a party already liable thereon may, with the consent of the holder, intervene and accept the bill *supra protest* for the honor of any party liable thereon, or for the honor of the person for whose account the bill is drawn.[4] This acceptance is termed "acceptance for honor."

§ 125. The method of accepting *supra protest* in England is said to be as follows: viz., the acceptor *supra protest* must personally appear before a notary public, with witnesses, and declare that he accepts the protested bill in honor of the drawer or indorser, as the case may be, and that he will

[1] Big. Bills and Notes, 61.

[2] Baring *v.* Clark, 19 Pick. 220.

[3] R. L. ch. 73, §§ 178 to 187 inclusive.

[4] R. L. ch. 73, § 178. "The acceptance for honor may be for part only of the sum for which the bill is drawn, and where there has been an acceptance for honor for one party, there may be a further acceptance by a different person for the honor of another party."

Following the law of England, in Massachusetts an acceptance for honor *supra protest* must be in writing and indicate that it is an acceptance for honor; must be signed by the acceptor for honor; and, in the absence of an express statement for whose honor it is satisfy the same at the appointed time; and then he must subscribe the bill with his own hand, thus: "Accepted, *supra protest*, in honor of A. B.," etc., or, as it is more usual, "Accepts, S. P." And a general acceptance, *supra protest*, which does not express for whose honor it is made, is considered as made for the honor of the drawer.[1]

Forms.

Act of Honor on Acceptance [to be written at the foot of the Protest].

Afterwards before me, the said Notary, and witnesses, appeared Messrs. A. B. & Co. of London, merchants, and declared that they would accept the bill of exchange before protested under protest, for the honor and upon the account of the C. D. Bank, Berlin, the second indorsers on the said bill.

Holding the second indorsers and all others concerned always bound and obliged to indemnify them, the said appearers for their said acceptance, and in case of payment by them for their reimbursement in due form of law, and according to the custom of merchants.

Principal	£100	0	0	Which I attest,
Notarial Charges		13	0	E. F.,
	£100	13	0	Notary Public.[2]

made, is deemed to be for the honor of the drawer. R. L. ch. 73, §§ 179, 180.

[1] Byles on Bills, 267.

[2] See Brooke's Notary, 173.

Act of Honor on Acceptance, supra protest, by a Third Person for the Honor of the Drawer [or Indorser].[1]

On the day of , one thousand nine hundred and , I., R. B., Notary Public, duly admitted and sworn, practising at , in the county of , and in the United Kingdom of Great Britain and Ireland, do hereby certify, that the original bill of exchange, for five hundred pounds, of which a copy is on the other side written, (now protested for non-acceptance,) was this day exhibited [*or* exhibited by me] unto E. F., one of the firm of E. F. and Company, who declared that the said firm would accept the said bill *supra protest*, for the honor of the drawer [*or* of G. H., the indorser;] holding the drawer [*or*, the said indorser and the drawer] and all other proper persons, responsible to the said firm for the said sum, and for all interest, damages, and expenses incident thereto; I have, therefore, granted this notarial act of honor accordingly.

Which I attest,

{ SEAL. } R. B.,
Notary Public.

§ 126. As to the contract of the acceptor for honor touching protest, it only remains to be said that he is liable to the holder and to all parties to the bill subsequent to the party for whose honor he has accepted; and that he engages that he will, on due presentment, pay the bill according to the

[1] Brooke's Notary, 176.

terms of his acceptance, provided it shall not have been paid by the drawee, and provided also, that it shall have been duly presented for payment and protested for non-payment and notice of dishonor given to him. When, therefore, a dishonored bill has been accepted for honor *supra protest* (or contains a reference in case of need), it must be protested for non-payment before it is presented for payment to the acceptor for honor (or referee in case of need).[1]

§ 127. "Reference in case of need" is usual on the Continent of Europe, and is recognized in England and America. When the drawer has any apprehension that the drawee will either not accept or not pay the bill, he may as a matter of precaution, to prevent the expenses and inconveniencies resulting from a return of the bill, require the holder to apply to a third person named in the bill for that purpose. This third person is called the referee in case of need. The holder is bound to apply to the party thus pointed out, and he may accept and pay the bill without previous protest, in which respect he differs from an acceptor *supra protest.* The usual form is, "*In case of need apply to Messrs.* , *at* ;" or, as the French say, "*Au besoin chez Messrs.* , *à* ;" and is written in the corner of the bill, under the drawee's

[1] Where a bill payable after sight is accepted for honor, its maturity is calculated from the date of the noting for non-acceptance, and not from the date of the acceptance for honor. R. L. ch. 73, § 183.

address. If the party so designated pays the bill he may recover the amount from the drawer. It would seem, however, that the introduction of these words rather imports a fear that the bill will not be regularly accepted or paid, and therefore tends to diminish the credit which might otherwise be attached to the bill without such desire being expressed.[1]

§ 128. When the bill is dishonored by the acceptor for honor, it must be protested for non-payment by him.[2]

PAYMENT FOR HONOR.

§ 129. Where a bill has been protested for non-payment, any person may intervene and pay it *supra protest* for the honor of any person liable thereon or for the honor of the person for whose account it was drawn. The payment for honor *supra protest*, in order to operate as such, and not as a mere voluntary payment, must be attested by *a notarial act of honor*, see the following sections, which may be appended to the protest or form an

[1] Chitty on Bills, * 165.

[2] Presentment for payment to the acceptor for honor (unless delay is excused by the Statute) must be as follows: (1) If it is to be presented in the place where the protest for non-payment was made, it must be presented not later than the day following its maturity; (2) If it is to be presented in some other place than that where it was protested, then it must be forwarded, except as the Statute otherwise provides, within a reasonable time. R. L. ch. 73, § 185.

extension to it. This *notarial act of honor* must be founded on a declaration made by the payer for honor, or by his agent in that behalf, declaring his intention to pay the bill for honor, and for whose honor he pays.[1] The Statute, which thus engrafts upon the law of Massachusetts the English doctrine of payment for honor, a doctrine which does not prevail to the extent of custom in this country,[2] is not founded upon the English common law, but is in accord with a provision of the general law merchant of England, introduced to aid the credit and circulation of bills of exchange.[3]

FORMS.

Act of Honor on Payment [to be written at the foot of the Protest].

Afterwards, on the day of , in the year aforesaid, before me, the said Notary, and witnesses, appeared A. B. of Boston aforesaid, merchant, and declared that he would pay the bill of exchange before protested under protest, for the honor and upon the account of the C. D. Bank, New York, the second indorsers on the said bill.

Holding, nevertheless, the second indorsers and all others concerned always bound and obliged for reim-

[1] R. L. ch. 73, §§ 188, 189, 190.
[2] Big. Bills and Notes, 276.
[3] Byles on Bills, 272.

bursement in due form of law and according to the custom of merchants.

Principal	$	Which I attest,
Notarial charges	.	E. F.,
	$.	Notary Public.

Received the day of , 1903, from A. B., the sum of , the amount of the said bill and notarial charges thereon.

(To be signed on behalf of the holders.)

Act of Honor on Payment supra protest, by a Firm of Third Persons, for the Honor of the Drawers and Indorsers.

COMMONWEALTH OF MASSACHUSETTS.[1]

[Name of County] } ss.

On the day of , one thousand nine hundred and , I., R. B., Notary Public, duly admitted and sworn, and practising in said county and in the town [*or* city] of B., do hereby certify, that the original bill of exchange for five hundred dollars, of which a copy is on the other side written, (now protested for non-payment), was this day exhibited to C. D. of B. , one of the firm of C. D. and Company, who declared [*or* declared before me] that the said firm would pay the amount of the said bill, *supra protest*, for the honor of E. F. and Company, the drawers, and G. H. and Company, the indorsers, holding the

[1] Brooke's Notary, 180.

drawers and the said indorsers, [*and* all prior indorsers, *if there are such*] and all other proper persons, responsible to them, the said C. D. and Company, for the said sum, and for all interest, damages and expenses; I have therefore granted this notarial act of honor accordingly.

Which I attest,

{ SEAL. }

R. B.,
Notary Public.

§ 130. The law merchant, as to payment *supra protest*, does not extend to promissory notes, which are not, like bills of exchange, instruments calculated or intended for circulation all over the globe. Whoever, therefore, pays a note for another person, without authority, express or implied, does so at his peril.[1]

FEES FOR PROTESTING.

§ 131. The fees of notaries public shall be as follows: For the protest of a bill of exchange, order, draft or check for non-acceptance or non-payment, or of a promissory note for non-payment, if the amount thereof is five hundred dollars or more, one dollar; if it is less than five hundred dollars, fifty cents; for noting the non-acceptance or non-payment of a bill of exchange, order, draft or check, or the non-payment of a promissory note,

[1] Byles on Bills, 274. *Contra*, that the payment for honor of promissory notes, though not common, is recognized in England, Brooke's Notary, 101 *n*. [3d ed].

seventy-five cents; and for each notice of the non-acceptance or non-payment of a bill, order, draft, check or note, given to a party liable for the payment thereof, twenty-five cents; but the whole cost of protest, including necessary notices and the record, if the bill, order, draft, check or note is of the amount of five hundred dollars or more, shall not exceed two dollars, and if it is less than five hundred dollars, shall not exceed one dollar and fifty cents; and the whole cost of noting, including recording and notices, shall in no case exceed one dollar and twenty-five cents.[1] Probably a private individual who makes protest has no right to charge fees therefor.[2]

RATES OF DAMAGES ON PROTESTED BILLS.

§ 132. When a bill of exchange, drawn or indorsed within this Commonwealth and payable beyond the limits of the United States, is duly protested for non-acceptance or non-payment, the party liable on such bill shall, on due notice and demand, pay it at the current rate of exchange on the date of the demand, with interest from the date of the protest and damages at the rate of five per cent upon the principal, thereof; and the amount of principal, interest and damages, shall be in satisfaction of all charges, expenses and damages. In an

[1] R. L. ch. 204, § 31. Cf. Legg *v.* Vinal, 165 Mass. 555; and compare City Bank *v.* Cutter, 3 Pick. 414.

[2] Read *v.* Bank of Kentucky, 1 T. B. Monroe, 91.

action on a contract, other than a bill of exchange, for the payment of money beyond the limits of the United States, the amount to be recovered by the creditor shall be determined by the current rate of exchange on the date when such contract becomes due, with interest from such date.

§ 133. The rates of damages to be allowed upon a bill of exchange, duly protested for non-acceptance or non-payment, if drawn or indorsed within this Commonwealth, and payable at a place beyond its limits, but within the United States, shall, in addition to the principal thereof, with interest and costs, be as follows: if payable in Maine, New Hampshire, Vermont, Rhode Island, Connecticut, or New York, two per cent; in New Jersey, Pennsylvania, Maryland, or Delaware, three per cent; in Virginia, West Virginia, North Carolina, South Carolina, or Georgia, or in the District of Columbia, four per cent; and in any other part of the United States or in the territories thereof, five per cent.

§ 134. The rate of damages upon a bill of exchange or order for the payment of not less than one hundred dollars, drawn or indorsed within this Commonwealth and payable therein at a place not less than seventy-five miles distant from the place where it is drawn or indorsed, when such bill or order is not duly accepted or paid, shall be one per cent in addition to the principal thereof, with interest thereon.[1]

[1] R. L. ch. 73, §§ 9, 10, 11, 12.

CHAPTER IV.

POWERS APART FROM STATUTE — *Continued.*

PART II.

NOTING AND EXTENDING OF MARINE PROTESTS.

(*a*) *Ship Protests Defined.*

§ 135. Another important act now recognized in this Commonwealth as pertaining to the office of notary public, apart from statute, is the noting and extending of marine protests.[1] A protest, in maritime matters, has been described as a declaration in writing, drawn up and attested by a notary public, by the master of a merchant ship, his mate and part of the ship's crew, after a voyage in which the ship has suffered in her hull, rigging or cargo, to show that such damage did not happen through any neglect or misconduct on their part.[2]

[1] Opinion of the Justices, 150 Mass. 586.

[2] Admiral Smyth's "Sailors' Word Book."

"A protest is a declaration, on oath, by the master of the circumstances attending the loss of his vessel, intending to show that the loss occurred by the perils of the sea, and concluding with a protestation against any liability of the owner to the freighters." *Curia, per* Frost, J., in Cudworth *v.* S. C. Ins. Co., 4 Rich. L. R. 416 [1851].

The protest is seldom made by the master alone; if it were, he

§ 136. Ship protests are most useful and important documents, especially in matters connected with the adjustment of losses in marine insurance, and in the calculation of general averages.[1] Their use and design seem to be chiefly to authenticate the fact of a loss to the insurer and all concerned, and to repel any inference unfavorable to the owner, from neglect to record, at the earliest time, a statement of the fact and cause of the loss.[2] Failure to protest is regarded with grave suspicion by the courts, especially in cases of salvage.[3] Nothing *said* by the captain can countervail his protest.[4] Protests should be prepared with impartiality, attention, and care; and masters must avoid the mistake, sometimes made, of employing persons to prepare these documents who are not notaries.

(*b*) "*Noting*" *the Protest.*

§ 137. When a vessel arrives at her port of destination, or at some intermediate port, after a

might be tempted to color his uncontradicted story in favor of his own side of the case, especially if he were a part owner, as sometimes happens. But although some of the crew join in the declaration, the act is that of the master. Cudworth *v.* S. C. Ins. Co., 4 Rich. L. R. 416. Marsh. Ins. 715. That some of the crew should join, Richette *v.* Stewart, 1 Dal. 317.

1 Brooke's Notary, 113.

2 Cudworth *v.* S. C. Ins. Co., 4 Rich. L. R. 416.

3 Dr. Lushington in The Emma, 2 W. Robinson's R. 315.

4 Campbell, Harvey & Co. *v.* Ship Alknomac, Bee's R. 124.

voyage in which she has suffered loss or damage "in hull, rigging, or cargo," the master usually goes to a notary public and causes a note or entry of protest to be made. This act is called "*noting the protest*," or "entering a note of protest," and is usually done as soon as the vessel enters port, or within twenty-four hours after.[1] Indeed, many prudent shipmasters make it a rule to enter a note of protest at the end of every considerable voyage, irrespective of accidents.

§ 138. The practice of noting a protest seems to have originated in the port of London, where shipmasters seldom did more in the first instance than have their intention to protest noted, or entered as they at first called it, before a notary public, instead of giving notice, according to the practice of Hamburg, to the consignees, importing a fear that the cargo was injured, and inviting them to inspect the stowage of it before it should be discharged.[2]

§ 139. The note or entry should contain the names of the vessel, the master, and the port whence she sailed; the dates of her departure and arrival; the nature of her cargo; and a statement of the accidents that caused the loss or damage.

§ 140. If the master has for good cause delayed to note the protest until after the usual time, it is customary to add to the noting or entry a short

1 Brooke's Notary, 112.
2 Fleming *v.* Marine Ins. Co., 3 W. and S 144.

statement giving the reason. The noting must bear the true date.[1]

Blank Form of Note of Protest.

COMMONWEALTH OF MASSACHUSETTS,

COUNTY OF SUFFOLK,

Boston,.........................19 .

Personally appeared.................................., Master of the ...., of................................, of the burden of ....Tons or thereabouts, and declared that he sailed from the port of........................, on................................, with a cargo of........................, bound to................................, and arrived..................................

Wherefore, he now Notes this Protest, to be extended if necessary

(Signed.)

....

Certified copies contain in addition the following: —

Know all men, that the above is a true and faithful copy of the original Note for Protest of Capt. ....now of record in my office.

Witness my hand and Notarial Seal this ....day of...............A. D. 19 .

[1] Brooke's Notary, 112, 113.

Completed Form of Entry of Note of Protest.

COMMONWEALTH OF MASSACHUSETTS.

COUNTY OF SUFFOLK } ss. CITY OF BOSTON.

On this first day of April, 1903, before me, Learned Sprague, a Public Notary, duly commissioned and sworn, dwelling in the City of Boston, personally came Simeon Tarsides, Master of the Steamship called the Runnymede, of West Hartlepool, of the burthen of three thousand six hundred seventy-eight tons, or thereabouts, laden with a cargo of general merchandise, and saith that he sailed from Liverpool, England, on the fourteenth day of March last, bound for Boston and arrived at this Port of Boston, the thirty-first day of March, 1903, but fearing damage, enters his protest in due form of law.

Before me SIMEON TARSIDES, *Master.*
LEARNED SPRAGUE,
Notary Public.

[If a certified copy of the above original is required, it may bear the following certification.]

COUNTY OF SUFFOLK } ss. CITY OF BOSTON.

I, Learned Sprague, a Public Notary, in and for the County of Suffolk, and Commonwealth of Massachusetts, duly commissioned and sworn, dwelling in said County and practising in the City of Boston, do certify the above to be a true and exact copy of an Original Protest on record in my office.

In my testimony whereof, I have hereunto set my hand and seal this first day of April, one thousand nine hundred and three.

{ SEAL } LEARNED SPRAGUE, *Notary Public.*

(c) "*Extending*" *the Protest.*

§ 141. A protest need not be extended by the notary in whose office it was noted. When it becomes necessary or expedient to have a protest extended, or written out in proper form, the document should be drawn up by any fully qualified notary, who will prepare it from entries in the log book and from information supplied by the master, officers, and crew.[1]

§ 142. The instrument of protest as drawn up by a notary consists of four parts: (1) the narrative or statement of facts and events; (2) the protestation; (3) the oath (or in England by Statute the declaration) of the master, officers, and crew; and (4) the attestation of the notary.[2]

§ 143. The narrative should be prepared with great care, and the information supplied to the notary should be absolutely consistent and accurate, for the protest may afterwards be given in evidence against the master and crew.[3]

[1] Brooke's Notary, 114. [2] Ibid., 114.

[3] Christian *v.* Coombe, 2 Esp. 490; Senat *v.* Porter, 7 T. R. 158; R. *v.* Scriveners Co., 10 B. & C. 511; The Betsey Caines, 2

§ 144. The protestation should not be long drawn out. A short, clear statement suffices. Thus, "The appearers, X, Y, and Z, do protest, and I, the undersigned notary, do also protest against the bad weather, gales, storms, accidents and occurrences mentioned in the foregoing statement (*or hereunto annexed*), and all loss or damage occasioned thereby."[1]

§ 145. The protest concludes with an attestation or certificate under the hand and seal of the notary, to the effect that the oath (or in England declaration) and protest were executed in due form of law.[2] Following is an approved form of an extended protest:

Blank Form of Extended Protest.

UNITED STATES OF AMERICA.

COMMONWEALTH OF MASSACHUSETTS.

SUFFOLK, ss. CITY OF BOSTON.

By this Public Instrument of Protest, be it known and made manifest, to all whom it doth or may concern, that on this day of , in the year of

Hagg. 28; Brig May Queen *v.* Merrimac, Newberry's Adm. R. 464.

[1] Brooke's Notary, 114. [2] Ibid., 115.

our Lord , before me, , a Notary Public, duly commissioned and sworn, and practising in Boston, personally came and appeared , Master of the , belonging to the Port of , of the burthen of tons, or thereabouts; and with him also came , of and belonging to the said , who being severally sworn, did declare and depose, that the said , being laden with a cargo of , they, the said appearers, made sail and departed in and with the said , from the Port of , bound to , on the day of , in the year . That in the prosecution of said voyage nothing material occurred until

That on the day of , the said first-named deponent having arrived at , did, within twenty-four hours thereafter, note for protest, before , to be extended if occasion should require. And the said appearers did further severally declare that the said at the time of her departure from , as aforesaid, was tight, staunch, and strong; had her hatches well and sufficiently caulked and covered; was well and sufficiently manned, provided and furnished with all things needful and necessary for said voyage; and that during the said voyage the said appearers and the residue of the crew used their utmost endeavors to preserve the said and her cargo from damage.

And therefore the said did declare to protest, and by these Presents he doth *solemnly protest* against all and every person or persons whomsoever it doth or may concern; and doth declare that all damages, losses, and detriments that have happened to the said and her cargo, are, and of right ought to be, borne by the Merchants and Freighters interested, or their respective Underwriters, or whomsoever else it doth or may concern, by way of average or otherwise, the same having occurred as before set forth, and not by or through the insufficiency of the Vessel, the neglect of him the said appearer, or either of the Mariners belonging to said Vessel.

In witness whereof, the said appearers have hereunto subscribed their names, in presence of me, the said Notary.

All which matters and things were declared, alleged, and affirmed before me the said Notary.

In Testimony Whereof, I have hereunto set my hand and affixed my official Seal.

{ SEAL } *Notary Public.*

Certified copies contain in addition the following:

COMMONWEALTH OF MASSACHUSETTS,
SUFFOLK, SS.

The foregoing Instrument is a true copy of the original Protest in my office.

In testimony whereof, I hereunto set my hand and seal.

{ SEAL } *Notary Public.*

Completed Form of Extended Protest.

UNITED STATES OF AMERICA.

COMMONWEALTH OF MASSACHUSETTS.

SUFFOLK, SS. CITY OF BOSTON.

By this Public Instrument of Protest Be it Known and made Manifest to all whom it doth or may concern, That on this twenty-fourth day of December in the year of our Lord one thousand nine hundred and two before me, John Marshall, a Notary Public, duly commissioned and sworn, personally came and appeared Joshua T. Snow, Master of the bark "Dancing Wave" belonging to the Port of New Bedford of the burthen of nine hundred and ninety-seven tons or thereabouts; and with him also came Samuel Saltmarsh, chief mate, and Billow Brown, carpenter, of and belonging to the said bark "Dancing Wave," who being severally sworn, did declare and depose, that the said bark "Dancing Wave," being laden with a cargo of sugar, they, the said appearers, made sail and departed in and with the said bark "Dancing Wave," from the Port of Samarang, Java, bound to St. Helena for orders on the twenty-seventh day of July in the year one thousand nine hundred and two.

That in the prosecution of said voyage,
Nothing material occurred until

Sept. 12 and 13, about midnight a heavy N. W. gale; 4 A. M. wind changed suddenly to S. W. carrying away the main and fore lower top sails. Heavy sea running, endeavored to head ship to sea and carried away the middle jib. Nothing worthy of mention happened until

Oct. 2, arrived at St. Helena.

Oct. 7, sailed from St. Helena bound for Delaware Breakwater for orders.

Nov. 29, arrived at Delaware Breakwater.

Dec. 10, sailed for Boston.

Dec. 12, 8 A. M., heavy E., S. E. to S. wind, heavy sea running, found that bark was only seven miles from Long Island. Increased the sail in order to keep the vessel off shore. On account of carrying stress of sail, two lower topsails and four upper topsails were blown away. Weather moderated somewhat. Set new sails, but before sails could be set was blown back 70 miles. 8 P. M. St. Dukes Light bore W. ¾ N.

Dec. 13, 5 A. M., sighted Five Fathom Bank Light, Northeast side about four miles off. Set sail again to get vessel off lee shore and blew away two degallant sails, main sail and two jibs. Decided to put into Vineyard Haven. Nothing of importance occurred until

Dec. 17, arrived at Vineyard Haven. The ship having blown away so many of her principal sails that she was not in a condition to proceed around Cape Cod in the winter season and since to supply her with sails at Vineyard Haven would be expensive and would cause great delay, it was decided, for the interest of all concerned, that the cheapest and best way was to tow her from Vineyard Haven to Boston.

Dec. 20, proceeded to Boston in tow.

Dec. 22, midnight, arrived at Boston.

That on the seventeenth day of December, the said first-named deponent having arrived at Vineyard Haven, did, within twenty-four hours thereafter, note for Protest, before Adam Westgate to be extended, if occasion should require. And the said appearers did further severally declare that the said bark "Dancing Wave" at the time of her departure from Samarang, Java, as aforesaid, was tight, staunch, and strong; and her hatches well and sufficiently caulked and covered; was well and sufficiently manned, provided, and furnished with all things needful and necessary for said voyage; and that during the said voyage the said appearers and the residue of the crew used their utmost endeavors to preserve the said bark and her cargo from damage.

And therefore the said Josuha T. Snow did declare to protest, and by these Presents he doth solemnly protest against all and every person or persons whomsoever it doth or may concern and doth declare that all damages, losses, and detriments that have happened to the said bark "Dancing Wave" and her cargo, are, and of right ought to be, borne by the Merchants and Freighters interested, or their respective Underwriters, or whomsoever else it doth or may concern, by way of average or otherwise, the same having occurred as before set forth, and not by or through the insufficiency of the vessel, the neglect of him the said appearer, or either of the Mariners belonging to said vessel.

In Witness whereof the said appearers have hereunto subscribed their names, in presence of me, the said Notary.

Joshua T. Snow,
Samuel Saltmarsh,
Billow Brown.

All which matters and things were declared, alleged and affirmed before me, the said Notary.

In Testimony Whereof I have hereunto set my hand and affixed my official Seal,

{SEAL.} JOHN MARSHALL,
Notary Public.

§ 146. Protests may be noted and extended by United States consuls, and authorized forms are provided by the United States government.

Blank Forms of Consular Protests.

MARINE NOTE OF PROTEST.

Consular Service, U. S. A.,

Port of ,

, 190 .

On this day of , in the year of our Lord nineteen hundred and , before me, , of the United States of America for and the dependencies thereof, personally appeared , Master of the vessel called the of , of the burden of tons or thereabout, and declared that on the day of last past he sailed in and with the said ship from the port of , laden with , and arrived, in the ship, at on [1] , and having experienced boisterous weather on the voyage

hereby enters this Note of Protest accordingly, to serve and avail him hereafter, if found necessary.

Master.

Attested:

{ SEAL } of the United States.

MARINE EXTENDED PROTEST.

Ship , Master,

Consular Service, U. S. A.,

Port of ,

, 190 .

By this public instrument of declaration and protest be it known and made manifest unto all to whom these presents shall come or may concern, that on the day of , one thousand nine hundred and , before me, , of the United States of America for and the dependencies thereof, personally came and appeared , Master of

[1] Here insert the day and hour.

the ship or vessel called the , of , of the burden of tons or thereabouts, then lying in this port of laden with cargo, who duly noted and entered with me, the said , his protest, for the uses and purposes hereafter mentioned; and now, on this day, to wit, the day of the date hereof, before me, the said , again comes the said ,and requires me to extend this protest; and together with the said also come , Mate, , , Carpenter, and , Seamen, of and belonging to the said ship, all of whom, being by me duly sworn on the Holy Evangelists of Almighty God, did severally voluntarily, freely, and solemnly declare, depose, and state as follows, that is to say: That these appearers, on the day of , in their capacities aforesaid, sailed in and with the said from the port of , laden with , and bound to the port of ; that the said ship was then tight, staunch, and strong; had her cargo well and sufficiently stowed and secured; had her hatches well caulked and covered; was well and sufficiently manned, victualed, and furnished with all things needful and necessary for a vessel in the merchant service, and particularly for the voyage she was about to undertake; that[1]

And these said appearers, upon their oaths aforesaid, do further declare and say: That during the said voy-

[1] Here insert narrative of the facts of the voyage as they occurred, with full and minute particulars, with dates, latitude, longitude, etc.

age they, together with the others of the said ship's company, used their utmost endeavors to preserve the said and cargo from all manner of loss, damage, or injury. Wherefore the said , Master, hath protested, as by these presents I, the said , at his special instance and request, do publicly and solemnly protest, against all and every person and persons whom it doth or may concern, and against the winds, and waves, and billows of the seas, and against all and every accident, matter, and thing, had and met with as aforesaid, whereby and by reason whereof the said or cargo already has, or hereafter shall appear to have, suffered or sustained damage or injury. And do declare that all losses, damages, costs, charges, and expenses that have happened to the said or cargo, or to either, are and ought to be borne by those to whom the same by right may appertain by way of average or otherwise, the same having occurred as before mentioned, and not by or through the insufficiency of the said , her tackle or apparel, or default or neglect of this appearer, his officers, or any of his mariners.

Thus done and protested in the port of , this day of , in the year of our Lord one thousand nine hundred and .

{ SEAL }

In Testimony Whereof, these appearers have hereunto subscribed their names, and I, the said , have granted to the said Master this public instrument, under my hand and the seal of this , to serve and to avail him, and all others whom it doth or may concern, as need and occasion may require.

,

of the United States.

, Master.
, Mate.
, Carpenter.
, Seaman.
, Seaman.

§ 147. Brooke tells us that if there is no notary practising at the port into which a British vessel has put, it is usual for the master to note a protest before the British consul, vice-consul, or consular agent.[1] This statement seems too narrow. It is certainly customary in this country for foreign consuls generally to note and extend ship protests, even though a notary public is near. And such protests, while not usual at the port of Boston, are by no means uncommon. The author has an attested copy of one before him at the hour of writing, and he has just had cause to examine a ship protest noted by the British consul at Providence, Rhode Island, U. S. A., where there are practising numerous public notaries. If the noting is made before any of these consular officers, it is well for the master to keep a copy of it, marked or certified by the officer before whom it is made. No one but a notary is entitled to a fee for noting

[1] Brooke's Notary, 113; 52 Vict. ch. 10, § 6, as extended by 54 and 55 Vict. ch. 50, § 2; Hopkins, "The Port of Refuge," 27, 28.

a protest. If the protest is later "extended," or written out in proper form, the fact of noting should be mentioned in the extended protest.

(*d*) *Duty of Master to Protest.*

§ 148. By custom, a legal obligation is said to be imposed upon a master and crew to give full and true information respecting the circumstances and events of the voyage, and to join in making an accurate and impartial protest when requested by the owners or consignees to do so. Whether or not a master refusing to comply with the request would be guilty of a breach of legal duty, and hence liable to the owners or consignees for loss arising from his refusal is a grave question. It has been declared in England that a refusal or omission by the master to insert certain particulars in his protest, even from improper motives, does not give the merchant a cause of action against the ship, as the omission or refusal would not prevent him recovering against the underwriters.[1]

(*e*) *Value of the Protest as Evidence.*

§ 149. To what extent a marine protest is admissible in evidence is a matter of some dispute. The question usually arises in actions on policies of assurance, with reference to which it is here

[1] Dr. Lushington in The Santa Anna, 32 L. J. Adm. 198; Abbott on Shipping, 13th ed. 457. *Contra*, Brooke's Notary, 115.

considered. That the protest is not admissible on behalf of the plaintiff in such cases seems settled law.[1] There are some American decisions, it is true, that are otherwise;[2] but the weight of authority is overwhelmingly against them. The protest stands in the same position as any other declaration made in the interest of the party who offers it; his own self-concern stamps his statement with the seal of prejudice, and destroys its credibility.[3]

§ 150. The doubt comes in cases of the defendant. Is the protest *per se* admissible in his behalf? If not, what circumstances render it admissible?

§ 151. More than a century ago there was decided the great English case of Senat *v.* Porter,[4] which was believed to answer these questions. The plaintiff's agent showed to the defendant, an underwriter, the captain's protest containing an account of the loss of the ship insured, demanding payment. The defendant contended that the protest was made evidence by the plaintiff as a paper delivered by his agent to the defendant, containing

[1] Richelieu and O. Nav. Co. *v.* Ins. Co., 26 Fed. R. 596 [1886].

[2] Nixon *v.* Long, 1 Dallas, 6; Fleming *v.* Marine Ins. Co., 3 Watts and Serg. 144; Campbell *v.* Williamson, 2 Bay (S. C.), 237; Miller & Brown *v.* S. C. Ins. Co., 2 McC. 336. It is an interesting fact that the judges in the first named case were not members of the bar.

[3] Richelieu and O. Nav. Co. *v.* Ins. Co., 26 Fed. R. 596.

[4] 7 T. R. 158 [1797].

an account of the loss on which he rested his claim, and therefore it amounted to a declaration made by the plaintiff to the defendant of the facts on which he required payment. Lord Kenyon, C. J., said, "That the protest *per se* cannot be evidence is admitted. . . . The mere circumstance of Vaux's" (the agent's) "showing the protest to the defendant when he applied to him for payment surely cannot render the protest evidence in this case." This decision was soon followed by the case of Christian *v.* Coombe,[1] and was uniformly regarded by contemporary text-writers and judges as settling the law.[2]

§ 152. But it did not settle the law, at least on this side of the Atlantic. In a recent case, Richelieu and Ontario Navigation Co. *v.* Boston Marine Insurance Co.,[3] decided in 1886, Brown, J., at the trial before the U. S. Circuit Court, said, "It is not so clear, however, that the protest may not be put in evidence by the defendant, though the better-considered cases hold that it stands in the light of an ordinary admission made by an agent, which is not competent against the principal unless it be part of the *res gestae.* But where the protest is served with the proof of loss, and made, in part,

[1] 2 Esp. 489.

[2] 2 Parsons on Shipping, 489; Senat *v.* Porter, 7 T. R. 158; Christian *v.* Coombe, 2 Esp. 490. Scriba *v.* Ins. Co., 1 Wash. C. C. 408, n.; Lamalere *v.* Caze, 1 Wash. C. C. 473; Winthrop *v.* Union Ins. Co., 2 Wash. C. C. 7; Patterson *v.* Ins. Co., 3 Harris & J. 71.

[3] 26 Fed. R. 598.

the basis of the plaintiff's claim against the company, we think he should be held as so far making the statement his own that it should be admitted against him."

§ 153. The court here relied on the case of Atkins *v.* Elwell,[1] which was even stronger than the case at bar. In Atkins *v.* Elwell, an action was brought by the plaintiffs to recover damages sustained by the fraud of the defendant on the sale of a ship to them. After the purchase, the ship was sent by the plaintiffs to San Francisco; but encountering bad weather she put into Rio de Janeiro in distress, where a protest was made by the master before the consul. The defendant expressly denied making any representations as to the vessel's soundness, and offered in evidence the protest, as showing the statements of the master as to the soundness and condition of the ship at the time of the disaster. According to Lord Kenyon, the protest *per se* was inadmissible, and this great judge had declared stronger additional facts not strong enough to make the protest evidence. But the court held it admissible. "It was a solemn instrument, made by their [the plaintiffs'] agent, for their benefit, in the course of his duty. . . . Whatever weight it had, the defendants were entitled to, as the statements, adopted by the plaintiffs, and used by them for their benefit in one instance, could not be repudiated by them in another."

[1] 45 N. Y. 753.

§ 154. Until 1890, when the case of Richelieu and Ontario Navigation Co. *v.* Boston Marine Insurance Co. was finally passed upon by the United States Supreme Court, the tendency of the decisions unquestionably was to enhance the value of marine protests as evidence.

§ 155. But in 1890, Fuller, C. J., delivered the following opinion, relative to the above-mentioned decision of Brown, J., in the court below; "Undoubtedly the protest of the captain, so long as he was living, would not be evidence on one side or the other, unless to contradict him if he varied from it. . . . But it was admissible in this case, not on the ground of agency, but because it was made part of the proofs of loss, being directly referred to in the proofs in the statement that the vessel ran ashore." [1]

§ 156. Strikingly similar is this language to the uncited words of a famous author who wrote many years ago, under the narrowing influence of Senat *v.* Porter, above discussed: "A protest, though a very important document, is not admissible as evidence in chief, but may be used to contradict the testimony of the persons who signed it." [2] One can but feel that the return to the older rule is unfortunate.

§ 157. Whether or not Chief Justice Fuller's

[1] Richelieu and Ontario Nav. Co., *v.* Boston Marine Ins. Co. 136 U. S. 408, at 435.

[2] 2 Parsons on Shipping, 489.

brief statement will be considered as overturning for all time the carefully considered precedents that are *contra*, is a grave question. That the learned Chief Justice himself would wish his statement to be too literally interpreted may well be doubted. But irrespective of purpose, the words have been uttered, and to-day are law.

(*f*) *Value of Protests as Preliminary Proofs of Loss to Insurers.*

§ 158. The value of protests as evidence in court of the facts they contain must not be confused with their value as preliminary proofs of loss in cases of insurance.

§ 159. Policies often stipulate that the insurers shall not be bound to pay the loss until a certain period elapses, which is usually sixty days or ninety days after proof of loss.[1] Thus, in the marine policies of the China Mutual Insurance Company in general use at the date of publication of this work, we find these words:

"Proofs of loss and all bills of expenses must be approved by the agent of the Company if there be one at or near the place where the loss occurs or the expenses are incurred, or if there be none in the vicinity, by the correspondent of the National Board of Marine Underwriters of New York, or Board of Marine Underwriters of Boston, and such agent or corres-

[1] 2 Parsons on Marine Ins. 473.

pondent must have a voice in the selection of members of all Boards of Survey. *Losses shall be paid in sixty days after this Company shall receive proof and adjustment thereof, together with proofs of interest in property insured, the amount of the premium note without discount if unpaid, and all sums due this Insurance Company from the insured, when such loss becomes due, being first deducted, and all sums coming due being first paid or secured to the satisfaction of the President and Directors, they discounting interest for anticipating payment.*"

§ 160. The first question is, What is meant by proof of loss? The insurers are not bound to pay at all without proof of loss; but when we say this, we mean that they are not bound to pay unless there be sufficient evidence of the loss to charge them with the liability, and, if need be, found a judgment against them. But this is certainly not the meaning of the phrase "proof of loss" in this stipulation. Much less than legal and complete proof is sufficient to begin the period at the end of which the insurers are bound to pay. The clause has always been, both in practice and adjudication, liberally construed. It refers simply to *preliminary* proof of loss.

§ 161. Briefly, preliminary proof must be all which the insured then possesses, and it must be sufficient to give the insurers such information as would enable them "to form some estimate of their rights and liabilities before they are bound to pay."

The insurer is undoubtedly entitled to all the evidence, or documents, which the insured has.[1]

§ 162. A difference, more apparent than real, seems to exist in the decisions concerning the value of marine protests as preliminary proofs of loss. Some of the best statements are quoted here. The protest "is the usual evidence when it can be obtained."[2] "A mariner's protest is only one of the preliminary proofs of loss which the assured is bound, by custom or the terms of the contract, to furnish the insurer before compensation can be demanded."[3] "The insured is bound to offer, as his preliminary proofs, such documentary proofs in his possession as are usually required in adjusting a partial loss; that is, the protest, bill of lading, and invoice, or such equivalent proofs as the nature of the case is susceptible of. . . . The burden of producing these proofs rests on the assured."[4] "Usually the insured gives to the insurer the protest of the master, the surveys and all communications which have

[1] 2 Parsons on Marine Ins. 473–476. "The question of the admissibility of any document in an action on the policy does not bear upon this question (*i.e.*, the question of its competency as a preliminary proof of loss); for if a document be material, in reference to the information which the insurers ought to have, they are entitled to it, though it would be legally inadmissible as evidence at the trial."

[2] Munson *v.* N. E. Marine Ins. Co., 4 Mass. 88.

[3] Fleming *v.* Marine Ins. Co., 3 W. and S. 144.

[4] Allegre *v.* Maryland Ins. Co., 6 H. and J. 408; 14 Am. Dec. 289; Patterson *v.* Same, 3 H. and J. 71.

been received from him or from any quarter, and if the insurance be on the cargo, the bill of lading and invoice should be given."[1] All of these definitions subsequent to the first, however, agree with the first that the protest is of prime importance as preliminary proof of loss, although it is not the only preliminary proof.

(*g*) *When the Protest must be Noted and Extended.*

§ 163. Having determined the real importance of the protest, we are brought to consider at what time it must be made. Whether or not the master must note a protest at the first port reached after a disaster to his ship is a question which has caused some conflict of authority. The older cases hold it necessary to protest as soon as possible, in order to prevent the collusion[2] and abuses[3] that may come from long delay, and in order that the document may be executed while the facts are fresh in the master's mind.

§ 164. But to-day, it is asserted that while "it is a useful and proper precaution for a master of a vessel to note a protest on his arrival at the first port — when it is in his power to do so — in all cases where an accident has occurred, or any

1 2 Parsons on Marine Ins. 475.

2 Richette *v.* Stewart, 1 Dal. 317 [1788].

3 Boyce *v.* Moore, 2 Dal. 196.

injury been sustained, or any possibility thereof, it is not an indispensable duty, without which the carrier cannot be relieved of liability."[1] The failure thus promptly to act simply casts something of suspicion over the affair.[2]

§ 165. Moreover, it has not always been clear as to whether a master is bound to note a protest within twenty-four hours after his craft is moored. Such was the rule in France formerly, if it be not the rule there to-day: [3] and such has been declared to be the law in the United States,[4] but, it would seem, erroneously.[5]

§ 166. The "twenty-four hour" doctrine here discussed was enunciated in Pennsylvania to aid insurance companies sued on marine policies. For by a peculiar rule of evidence there, the protest (which is solely the plaintiff's act and hence completely within his control) is admissible on behalf of the plaintiff in an action on a marine policy.

1 Hunt *v.* The Cleveland, 6 M'Lean, 76 [1853].

2 The Charlotte Caroline, 1 Dodson's Adm. 192 at 195. Sir William Scott: "Now I must say, that in my opinion, it is much to the disadvantage of that protest that it was not made immediately on his arrival at a port in Denmark . . . It was his (the master's) duty to have taken the first opportunity of putting the facts on record."

3 Richette *v.* Stewart, 1 Dal. 317 [1788].

4 Richette *v.* Stewart, 1 Dal. 317; Fleming *v.* The Marine Ins. Co., 3 W. and S. 144; Lewis on Shipping, 89; Jacobsen's Sea Laws, 373; cf. The Charlotte Caroline, 1 Dodson's Adm. R. 192.

5 Ins. Co. *v.* Francia, 9 Barr (Pa.), 390; Com. Ins. Co. *v.* Sennett, 41 Pa. St. 166.

§ 167. To remedy this injustice, the court in Fleming *v.* The Marine Ins. Co.[1] declared that "it is a mistake to suppose that a protest noted in time may be extended afterwards. The better opinion seems to be, that it must be made, and consequently completed, if not within the twenty-four hours, yet certainly before the goods have been landed, or the condition of the cargo ascertained. The noting of a protest must not be taken for the material part of it, because it would still leave the framing of it open to be influenced by the condition of the goods when sent on shore. As then [in the case at bar] the act of protest was not concluded until the goods were landed, it was properly rejected as a document to show the cause of the loss."

§ 168. This case, however, was soon modified by Insurance Co. *v.* Francia,[2] where the protest of the master, not made within twenty-four hours after reaching port, was presented to the insurance office with the other preliminary proof. The protest was not offered or admitted as evidence to the jury, but simply as one of the usual documents exhibited to the underwriters to inform them of the details of the loss, and one whose absence is suspicious. It was objected that the protest, not being made within the twenty-four hours or as soon as possible thereafter, was white paper. Upon this objection,

[1] 3 W. and S. 144.

[2] 9 Barr (Pa.), 390.

Gibson, C. J., observed, "In Fleming *v.* The Marine Insurance Co., we certainly laid a strong hand on protests, under the idiosyncrasy of our system, of facts before a jury, not, however, to affect them as preliminary proofs. The rule for the latter is so liberally expounded as to require only the best evidence in the possession of the assured, as reasonable information, to enable the underwriters to form an estimate of their liability for the loss." [1]

§ 169. Probably the only effect to-day of a failure to note a protest within twenty-four hours after the vessel comes in, or as soon as possible thereafter, is to put the protest under a cloud of suspicion and doubt.[2] This outside of Pennsylvania, and possibly South Carolina, where the rule as to the admissibility of protests as evidence is the same as in Pennsylvania.

(*h*) *Effect upon Legal Rights of Insurer and Insured where there is Failure to Extend a Protest Promptly (with Special Reference to the Custom of the Port of Boston).*

§ 170. The custom at the Port of Boston is to note a protest within the twenty-four hours, if possible, but to extend it only when necessity requires, perhaps long after the noting. This on the theory

[1] Com. Ins. Co. *v.* Sennett, 41 Pa. St. 166.

[2] Sir W. Scott, in The Charlotte Caroline, 1 Dodson's Adm. 192, at 195.

that the ship is legally safe if the master notes a protest when damage is merely suspected, and extends it when the damage is actually ascertained.

§ 171. Query: In cases of insurance where it is difficult to prove loss by perils of the sea, is this custom altogether safe?

§ 172. It is clear that the value of a protest may vary in a given case. Thus, a forged protest, a protest made under duress, or a protest extended at the dictation of an insane master would be worthless.

§ 173. So the courts have said that a protest extended long after the noting is of less value than one made while the facts are fresh in the master's mind. Such a protest as the former is, as we have seen, an object of judicial suspicion.

§ 174. Conceive of a doubtful case where the issue is, Did the assured furnish the insurer with sufficient preliminary proofs of loss? The proof furnished is a noted and extended protest, upon the value of which the court is to pass. Obviously whether or not the protest is a good one may be determining for or against its offerer; and if the protest (through long delay in its extending) be tainted with suspicion, it may be controlling against him.

§ 175. Exactly to determine the attitude of the courts toward such a protest, we need only quote the words of two of England's greatest admiralty judges. Rt. Hon. Stephen Lushington, in The

Emma, a salvage case, said "Every protest is presumed to be made *recenti facto*, and to contain a statement of the transaction when the facts are fresh in the memories of the parties deposing to it, whereas the discussion and legal investigation of those facts, and of the evidence taken upon them, cannot be had until a much later period, when even those who are inclined to speak with the most perfect accuracy as to the nature and extent of the salvage services may find their memory fail them with respect to certain points. This is one reason why the production of the protest is required and ought to be observed."[1]

§ 176. Sir William Scott, of the English High Court of Admiralty, in the Charlotte Caroline: "Now I must say that in my opinion, it is much to the disadvantage of that protest that it was not made immediately on his [the master's] arrival at a port in Denmark. It was his duty to have taken the first opportunity of putting the *facts* on record."[2]

§ 177. We may well be certain that the courts will pay little deference to a custom of the mariners of a particular port, when that custom is abhorrent to existing law.

§ 178. It may be said in conclusion that the above view has been reached only after a careful examination of every decided case in England or

[1] 2 W. Robinson, 315.

[2] 1 Dodson's Adm. 192 at 195; Richette *v.* Stewart, 1 Dal. 317; Hunt *v.* The Cleveland, 6 M'Lean, 76.

America bearing upon the subject of marine protests. It is to be regretted that the scope of the present work forbids a more complete discussion of the authorities.

(*i*) *Expenses.*

§ 179. The master personally is not burdened with the expense of protest. In England the shipowner must, beyond doubt, pay for noting the protest, and probably for extending it, except if the owners or consignees of goods require the protest to be made, they must pay the notary, or tender the cost to the shipowners or master when the request is made. The owners or consignees are entitled to have the protest drawn up by their own notary.[1] Here, the custom is for the ship to pay

[1] Brooke's Notary, 115. Says a recent English author, "It was not doubted formerly, and it is still held by many, that the cost of extending the protest is one which falls on the shipowner. In cases of general average he recovers the expense from the various contributories. No doubt exists that the noting is at the owner's cost; but, latterly, a doctrine has been maintained by some owners and acted on, that the note of protest is all which the shipowner is called upon to provide at his own expense, and that the noting is a sufficient answer on his part to any claim for damage or short delivery of cargo; and that if consignees and owners of goods require the protest in its extended, that is, in its completed and useful form, they must themselves pay the cost of it. It is observable that this view, which many will look on as an innovation affecting the position and security of cargo proprietors, does not arise among the class of smaller shipowners, to whom the expense of a protest may be of some importance, but it is put forward by some of the

for the protest, and for the owners or consignees of the goods to pay for certified copies of the protest, if they desire them.

(*j*) *Delegation of Notarial Powers.*

§ 180. A notary cannot delegate his authority or functions. Brooke says he cannot "empower another person, except a *clerk* in his employment, to note or make protests or notarial instruments in his name.[1] It would seem that even this language is too broad, and that the same causes which operate to invalidate protest of commercial paper by a notary's clerk, operate to invalidate the noting and extending of marine protests by such a factotum.[2]

(*k*) *Other Protests.*

§ 181. In addition to ship protests, there are protests relating to other matters: *e.g.*, for refusing to sign proper bills of lading, for not providing a cargo, for not delivering goods, for detention,

wealthiest owners and most extensive steam companies. It may therefore be supposed that the refusal to provide an extended protest gratuitously by such influential parties is a considered step on their part. It is one which certainly interposes a practical difficulty in the way of the merchant or other claimant against the ship, in preventing his ascertaining by a recognized document the facts of his voyage." Hopkins, "The Port of Refuge," 28 [1882].

[1] Brooke's Notary, 116.

[2] Ocean Bank *v.* Williams, 102 Mass. 141.

for demurrage, for not signing a charter party, for the misconduct or intoxication of the captain, for the insufficiency or unseaworthiness of the vessel, and for many other irregularities relating to ships, cargoes, and mercantile matters. Protests of this character are said to be of great use in foreign countries in disputes with other parties residing abroad, and interested in ships or their cargoes.[1]

(*l*) *Fees.*

§ 182. The ordinary fee for noting a marine protest is fixed by custom at one dollar; and for extending such a protest, at ten dollars. But these fees vary in proportion to the work involved in noting or extending the protest.

(*m*) CERTIFICATES OF SURVEY.

§ 183. Connected to a certain extent with ship protests are the notarial certificates of surveys held on a vessel or cargo.

Form of Certificate of Survey.

UNITED STATES OF AMERICA.

TO THOMAS W. BROWN, FRED A. WHITE AND WALTER B. MEAD.

Gentlemen, — At the request of Captain Joshua T. Blow, master of bark "Dripping Sword," of Boston, Mass., you are hereby

[1] Brooke's Notary, 116.

{SEAL.} authorized and requested to examine said vessel as she now lies at Vineyard Haven in a damaged condition, she having been out in heavy gales of wind on passage from Samarang, Java, for Boston, via St. Helena & Delaware Breakwater.

Witness my hand and seal of office, this nineteenth day of December, A. D. 1902.

GEORGE B. CLIFFORD, *Notary Public.*

Pursuant to the foregoing request to us directed by George B. Clifford, a Notary Public for the Commonwealth of Massachusetts, the undersigned held a survey on bark "Dripping Sword" of Boston, Mass., damaged as aforesaid, and found as follows:

Lower and Upper Fore Topsails, Degallant Sails, Main Royal and Jibs torn and blown away. Iron Port on Starboard side washed away and lost. We recommend Captain Joshua T. Blow, to procure the services of a tugboat and tow Vessel to destination.

COMMONWEALTH OF MASSACHUSETTS.

DUKES COUNTY, SS. DECEMBER 19, A. D., 1902.

Personally appeared the above-named Thomas W. Brown, Fred A. White and Walter B. Mead, who signed the foregoing report in my presence, and made oath that the statements therein are true,

{SEAL.} In testimony whereof, I have hereunto set my hand and seal of office,

GEORGE B. CLIFFORD, *Notary Public.*

I certify that the foregoing is a true copy of the original on record in my office,

GEORGE B. CLIFFORD, *Notary Public.*

(*n*) RECORDS.

§ 184. The notary who notes and extends marine protests should keep a record book in which the original noting and extending is to be made, or at least should enter in his notarial book the fact of a protest, and the reasons given for making the protest. A common form is, "By this public act be it known to all whom it does concern, . . . wherefore the said . . . protested, and I, the said notary, do by these presents publicly protest."

§ 185. The notary's book is never given out. That is a record of the notary's office, made there for the benefit of all whom it may concern. The benefit of this record is secured to those concerned by issuing a transcript from the book, certified by the notary to be correct, and in no other way is the protest made available. The courts have said, "It could never be successfully contended that, to prove a marine protest in a court of admiralty, the notary must be examined upon a commission." [1]

§ 186. The notarial book should contain blank forms of the noting and of the extension thereof, to be filled out as occasion requires. Such a book may be compiled by reference to the blank forms herein given.[2]

[1] The Gallego, 30 Fed. R. 271.

[2] Courtesy of Theodore W. and Christopher Gore, average

[Act of March 2, 1799, c. 22, § 60, v. 1, p. 672.

DISTRESS OF WEATHER.

§ 187. "If any vessel from any foreign port, compelled by distress of weather, or other necessity, shall put into any port of the United States, not being destined for the same, the master, together with the mate or person next in command, may, within twenty-four hours after her arrival, make protest in the usual form upon oath, before a notary public or other person duly authorized, or before the collector of the district where the vessel arrives, setting forth the cause or circumstances of such distress or necessity. Such protest, if not made before the collector, shall be produced to him, and to the naval officer, if any, and a copy thereof lodged with him or them. The master shall also, within forty-eight hours after such arrival, make report in writing to the collector, of the vessel and her cargo, as is directed hereby to be done in other cases. And if it appear to the collector, by the certificate of the wardens of the port, or other officers usually charged with, and accustomed to ascertain the condition of vessels arriving in distress, if any, or by the certificate of two reputable merchants, to be named for that purpose by the collector, if there are no such wardens, or other

adjusters and notaries public, Boston. Courtesy of George M. Amerige, Esq., Secretary of Boston Board of Marine Underwriters.

officers duly qualified, that there is a necessity for unlading the vessel, the collector and naval officer, if any, shall grant a permit for that purpose, and shall appoint an inspector to oversee such unlading, who shall keep an account of the same, to be compared with the report made by the master of the vessel."] [1]

[1] Rev. Stat. of the U. S., Title XXXIV. ch. 5, sec. 2891.

CHAPTER V.

POWERS GIVEN BY STATUTE.

ACKNOWLEDGMENT OF DEEDS AND ADMINISTRATION OF AFFIDAVITS, ETC.

§ 188. Notaries public have like power as justices of the peace to administer oaths, and take acknowledgments of deeds and other instruments,[1] and may exercise their powers throughout the Commonwealth.[2]

§ 189. The acknowledgment of a deed must be by the grantors or one of them, or by the attorney who executes the deed, and the notary before whom the acknowledgment is made, who should be a person not appearing on the face of the deed to be interested as one of the parties or otherwise,[3] must indorse upon or annex to the deed a certificate of such acknowledgment;[4] and where the acknowledgment of a deed is taken and certified

[1] For example, certificates of limited partnerships, see R. L. ch. 71, § 5.

[2] R. L. ch. 17, § 1.

[3] Jones, Real Prop. §§ 1125, 1126.

[4] R. L. ch. 127, § 8.

by a notary public, his certificate need not be authenticated by his official seal.[1]

(*For forms of acknowledgment of deeds, see post* § 268.)

§ 190. Notaries public in this Commonwealth may take acknowledgments of deeds conveying real estate situated in certain of the other states and territories. These states and territories it would be unsafe to enumerate here, since the notarial authority referred to is purely statutory and hence liable to change. In the case of several states, the authority of the notary to take acknowledgments must be certified to before a clerk of court, under his seal. It is better in every case to use the notarial seal.

NOMINATION PAPER AFFIDAVITS.

§ 191. A notary public, when taking the oath of a signer of a nomination paper, as provided in section 144 of chapter 11 of the Revised Laws, must satisfy himself that the person to whom the oath is administered is the person signing such nomination paper, and must so state in his attestation of said oath, under penalty of a fine of not less than ten or more than fifty dollars.[2]

[1] Farnum *v.* Buffum, 4 Cush. 260.
[2] R. L. ch. 11, §§ 145, 397.

FORECLOSURE AFFIDAVITS.

§ 192. The certificate of an entry made for the purpose of foreclosing a mortgage for breach of condition thereof may be sworn to before a notary public.[1]

OPENING OF SAFETY DEPOSIT VAULTS.

§ 193. A notary public who is not an officer or in the general employ of the corporation is required to be present together with the president, treasurer or superintendent of a corporation organized under the laws of this Commonwealth for the purpose of letting vaults, safes and other receptacles, when any box or safe in the vaults of such corporation is opened because of non-payment of the rent. The notary public must remove the contents of such safe or box, make a list of the same and seal up such contents in a package and mark thereon the name of the person in whose name such safe or box stood on the books of such corporation and his address as stated on said books, and such package must, in the presence of said notary and of said president, treasurer or superintendent, be placed in one of the storage vaults of such corporation. The notary public must set forth his proceedings, including the list of the contents of said box or safe and his estimate of the

[1] R. L. ch. 187, § 2; see Murphy *v.* Murphy, 145 Mass. 224.

total value of the contents, in his own handwriting and under his official seal, in a book kept by the corporation for the purpose. The notary public must swear to this statement before a justice of the peace.[1]

PROOFS IN INSOLVENCY.

§ 194. A notary public may take proofs in insolvency. The creditor in person, or if he is disabled by absence from the Commonwealth, illness or other cause from proving his claim, his agent or attorney testifying to the best of his knowledge and belief, must make an oath before the notary public in substance as follows: —

I, , do swear that , of , by [*or* against] whom proceedings in insolvency have been instituted, at and before the date of such proceedings was and still is justly and truly indebted to me in the sum of , for which sum or any part thereof I have not, nor has any other person to my use, to my knowl edge or belief, received any security or satisfaction whatever, beyond what has been disposed of agreeably to law. And I do further swear that said claim was not procured by me for the purpose of influencing the proceedings in this case. And I do further swear that I have not directly or indirectly made or entered into any bargain, arrangement or agreement, express or implied, to sell, transfer or dispose of my claim, or any part of my claim, against said debtor, nor have directly or in-

[1] R. L. ch. 116, § 38.

directly received or taken, or made or entered into any bargain, arrangement, or agreement, express or implied, to take or receive directly or indirectly any money, property, or consideration whatsoever to myself, or to any person or persons to my use or benefit, under or with any understanding or agreement, express or implied, whereby my vote for assignee or my assent to the debtor's discharge is or shall be in any way affected, influenced, or controlled, or whereby the proceedings in this case are or shall be affected, influenced or controlled.[1]

SAVINGS BANK AFFIDAVITS.

§ 195. Notaries public may take affidavits under their seals, to be annexed to copies from the records, books and accounts of a savings bank and institution for savings, incorporated under the laws of this Commonwealth, and these then become competent evidence in all cases equally with their originals. The affidavit must set forth that the affiant is the officer having charge of the original records, books and accounts, and that such copy is true and correct, and is full, so far as it relates to the subject-matter therein referred to.[2]

MAY BELONG TO LICENSING BOARDS.

§ 196. Notaries public are not disqualified, by being such, from serving as members of licensing

[1] R. L. ch. 163, §§ 39, 40, 41.
[2] R. L. ch. 113, § 54.

boards appointed in cities to grant licenses for the sale of intoxicating liquors.[1]

MAY ADMINISTER OATHS OF MUSTER.

§ 197. If a soldier re-enlisting in the volunteer militia of this Commonwealth is at such a distance from his command that he cannot be mustered in by the mustering officer of his regiment, battalion, naval brigade or corps, he may, with the approval of his proper commanding officer, to secure continuous service, take the oath of muster before a notary public.[2]

Form of Muster Oath.

I,   , do solemnly swear that I will bear true faith and allegiance to the Commonwealth of Massachusetts, and will support the constitution thereof; and I do also solemnly swear that I will faithfully observe and obey all laws and regulations for the government of the volunteer militia of said Commonwealth, and the orders of all officers elected or appointed over me. I do also solemnly swear that I will support the Constitution of the United States. So help me God.

Sworn to before me,

, Notary Public.

[1] R. L. ch. 100, § 3.
[2] R. L. ch. 16, § 72.

MAY ADMINISTER OATHS AS TO TAX LISTS.

§ 198. A very interesting statute, relating to the verification under oath of tax lists by the persons bringing them in, provides that if the person bringing such list is absent from the place in which the tax is to be assessed during the whole period when such oath may be made, the oath may be administered by a notary public, whose jurat *must* be duly authenticated by his seal.[1]

MAY GIVE NOTICE TO NON-RESIDENT OWNERS OF INSECURE BUILDINGS.

§ 199. If an owner of, or person interested in a building or structure which has been declared to be unsafe and dangerous under the provisions of chapter 104 of the Revised Laws, lives out of the Commonwealth, the notices provided for therein may be served upon him by a notary public, whose certificate of service under his notarial seal shall be sufficient evidence thereof.[2]

PENALTY FOR FORGING NOTARIAL DOCUMENTS.

§ 200. Whoever, with intent to injure or defraud, falsely makes, alters, forges or counterfeits a certificate, return or attestation of a notary

[1] R. L. ch. 12, § 43.
[2] R. L. ch. 104, § 9.

public, in relation to a matter wherein such certificate, return or attestation may be received as legal proof, or whoever with such intent utters and publishes as true such false, forged or altered instrument, knowing the same to be so, is liable to punishment by imprisonment in the state prison for not more than ten years or in jail for not more than two years.[1]

[1] R. L. ch. 209, §§ 1, 3.

PART II.

JUSTICES OF THE PEACE,

AND

SPECIAL COMMISSIONERS.

PART II.

JUSTICES OF THE PEACE

AND

SPECIAL COMMISSIONERS.

CHAPTER I.

ORIGIN AND APPOINTMENT.

ORIGIN.

§ 201. Prior to the year 1327 there were no justices of the peace in England,[1] although there were certain officers, like the judges of the king's bench, who by virtue of their official positions, were guardians of the peace; and certain local officers called conservators, wardens or keepers of the peace, who were elected by the people.[2] When the weak King Edward II was deposed by his wife Isabel, and his son Edward III placed upon the

[1] Jerome's Case, 4 Leon. 149. "To be a Justice of Peace doth not lye in Prescription; for no Justice of Peace was before the Statute 1 Ed. 3, and the beginning of them being known, Prescription cannot be."

[2] Bac. Abr. Tit. Justices of the Peace, 395.

throne, England was thrown into a state of civic restlessness, and the conservators of the peace elected by the people failed to quell the people's alarm. The new king felt that he must appoint his own guardians of the peace, if the peace was to be preserved. To enable him to act, legislation was necessary.[1] By Act of Parliament, 1 Edward III, Chapter 16, in the year 1327, it was provided as follows: "Also, for the better keeping and Maintenance of the Peace, the King willeth, That in every County good Men and lawful, which be no Maintainers of Evil Quarrels in the Country, shall be assigned to keep the Peace."[2] This Act neither gave any new powers nor extended the limits of the former authority. It simply took away the election of conservators of the peace from the people and placed it in the assignment of the crown.[3] These officers were still called, and in fact were no more than, conservators, wardens, or keepers of the peace, till the Statute 34 Edward III, Chapter 1, in the year 1360, gave them the power of trying felonies, and then they acquired the more honorable appellation of Justices.[4]

§ 202. In Massachusetts, justices of the peace originally had the power to try minor causes, both civil and criminal. But since the passage of the

[1] 1 Bl. Com. 349.
[2] 1 Ed. III, ch. 16.
[3] Bac. Abr. Tit. Justices of the Peace, 396.
[4] 1 Bl. Com. 349.

Acts of 1858, ch. 138, § 1, and the Acts of 1877, ch. 211, § 1, justices of the peace, as such, have no power to try cases, civil or criminal, nor have they any power to receive complaints or to issue warrants, except in certain cases. At the present time, therefore, their powers are very limited, and are confined to certain ministerial acts, which are strictly defined by statutes.

APPOINTMENT.

§ 203. All justices of the peace are nominated and appointed by the governor, by and with the advice of the council; and every such nomination must be made by the governor, and made at least seven days prior to such appointment.[1]

§ 204. It is much easier to obtain the appointment of justice of the peace than that of notary public. Any man who is more than twenty-one years of age, of good character, a citizen of the United States and a resident of Massachusetts, may be appointed. But if the applicant is not a counsellor at law, it is better to allege good reasons for the appointment, on the application.

§ 205. Although women cannot be appointed justices of the peace, still women who are twenty-one years of age may be appointed special commissioners, for a term of seven years, and have like powers as justices of the peace to administer oaths, to take depositions, affidavits, acknowledg-

[1] Mass. Const., Part. II. ch. ii. art. ix.

ments of deeds and other instruments, to issue summonses for witnesses, and to appoint appraisers in all cases. They are entitled to like fees as justices of the peace for like services.[1]

§ 206. If the name of a special commissioner is changed, her commission terminates, but she may be reappointed under her new name.[2]

§ 207. The applicant for the office of justice of the peace or special commissioner must fill out a blank, in form as shown below, which may be procured at the office of the secretary of the Commonwealth. The application must be signed by two reputable citizens of the Commonwealth, and be deposited in the executive office at the State House.

COMMONWEALTH OF MASSACHUSETTS.

To His Excellency the Governor:

I hereby petition for appointment to the office of

Justice of the Peace

for the Commonwealth of Massachusetts.

Residence[3] ....

Business address[4] ....

Occupation ....

I was born in .... Age ....

I desire the appointment for the following reasons: [state best reasons possible]

(Sign here.) ....

(The above blank must be filled out by the applicant and no one else.)

[1] R. L. ch. 17, § 5.
[2] R. L. ch. 17, § 6.
[3] Give city or town.
[4] Give street and number.

We certify that we are personally acquainted with the above-named applicant and consider him a man of high standing and character and in every way fitted for the appointment of Justice of the Peace.

....

....

Dated this ....

day of .... 190 .

(This certificate must be signed by at least two well-known persons.)

If the applicant was born in a foreign country, he must furnish proof that he is a citizen of the United States.

COMMONWEALTH OF MASSACHUSETTS.

To His Excellency the Governor:

I hereby petition for appointment to the office of

Special Commissioner

for the Commonwealth of Massachusetts.

Residence [1] ....

Business address [2] ....

Occupation ....

I was born in .... Age ....

I desire the appointment for the following reasons: [state best reasons possible]

(Sign here.) ....

(The above blank must be filled out by the applicant and no one else.)

We certify that we are personally acquainted with the above-named applicant. She is a resident of

[1] Give city or town. [2] Give street and number.

Massachusetts, more than twenty-one years of age, and of high standing and character.

....

....

Dated this..............................

day of..........................190 .

(This certificate must be signed by at least two well-known persons.)

§ 208. Before the delivery of a commission to a person appointed justice of the peace or special commissioner, he or she is required to pay to the secretary of the Commonwealth a fee of five dollars.[1]

§ 209. A person appointed by the governor to the office of justice of the peace or special commissioner will be notified of the appointment by the secretary of the Commonwealth, and the commission delivered to him or her, and if he or she does not, within three months after the date of such appointment, take and subscribe the oaths of office, the appointment will be void; and the secretary is required forthwith to notify him or her thereof, and require the return of the commission, and also to certify said facts to the governor.[2]

§ 210. The following oath must be taken and subscribed by every person appointed to the office of justice of the peace or special commissioner

[1] R. L. ch. 18, § 9.
[2] R. L. ch. 18, § 8.

before he or she enters upon the duties of the office, to wit —:

"I, A. B., do solemnly swear, that I will bear true faith and allegiance to the Commonwealth of Massachusetts, and will support the Constitution thereof. So help me, God."

Provided, that when any person is of the denomination called Quakers, and declines taking said oath, he may make his affirmation in the foregoing form, omitting the word "swear" and inserting, instead thereof, the word "affirm," and omitting the words, "So help me, God," and subjoining, instead thereof, the words, "This I do under the pains and penalties of perjury."[1]

§ 211. Justices of the peace are appointed, and their commissions issued, for the Commonwealth, and they have jurisdiction throughout the Commonwealth, except as provided in sections three and four of chapter 161 of the Revised Laws.[2] (See §§ 273, 274, *post.*)

§ 212. In order that the people may not suffer from the long continuance in place of any justice of the peace who shall fail of discharging the important duties of his office with ability or fidelity, all commissions of justices of the peace are made to expire and become void, in the term of seven years from their respective dates; and, upon the expiration of any commission, the same may, if neces-

[1] Mass. Const. Amend., Art. VI.

[2] R. L. ch. 161, § 1.

sary, be renewed, or another person appointed, as shall most conduce to the well-being of the Commonwealth.[1]

§ 213. The secretary of the Commonwealth is required to send by mail to every justice of the peace or special commissioner, a notice of the time of the expiration of his or her commission, not more than thirty nor less than fourteen days before such expiration.[2]

§ 214. Whoever presumes to act as a justice of the peace or special commissioner after the expiration of his or her commission, and after receiving notice of such expiration may be punished by a fine of not less than one hundred nor more than five hundred dollars.[3]

MAY HOLD OTHER OFFICES.

§ 215. The office of justice of the peace is not subject to the provisions regarding plurality of office. So that a person may be a justice of the peace, and at the same time hold any other office which is within the gift of the governor of the Commonwealth or that of the people.[4] A justice of the peace may hold the office of referee in

[1] Mass. Const., Part II. ch. iii. art. iii.

[2] R. L. ch. 5, § 8.

[3] R. L. ch. 210, § 34.

[4] Mass. Const., Part. II. ch. vi. art. ii. cl. 2; Amend., Art. VIII.

bankruptcy, or a judicial office under the laws of the United States.[1]

§ 216. The governor, with the advice and consent of the council, is required, from time to time, to designate and commission in the several counties a suitable number of justices of the peace as trial justices, and may at any time revoke such designation.[2]

EXEMPTION FROM WATCH DUTIES.

§ 217. Justices of the peace are exempt from watch and ward duties to which all male persons of the age of eighteen years or over not exempt are liable in their cities or towns.[3]

FALSELY ASSUMING TO BE A JUSTICE.

§ 218. Whoever falsely assumes or pretends to be a justice of the peace, or special commissioner, and acts as such, or requires a person to aid or assist him in a matter pertaining to the duty of such officer, may be punished by imprisonment for not more than one year, or by a fine of not more than four hundred dollars.[4]

[1] R. L. ch. 166, §§ 10, 11.

[2] R. L. ch. 161, § 6; Mead *v.* Bowker, 168 Mass. 234.

[3] R. L. ch. 31, § 6.

[4] R. L. ch. 210, § 33.

CHAPTER II.

DEPOSITIONS.

METHOD OF TAKING.

§ 219. If a witness or party whose testimony is wanted in a civil cause or proceeding pending in this Commonwealth lives more than thirty miles from the place of trial, or is about to go out of the Commonwealth and not to return in time for the trial, or is so ill, aged or infirm as to make it probable that he will not be able to attend at the trial, his deposition may be taken.[1]

§ 220. When a deposition is taken with a view to a future trial, it is always subject to contingencies. Therefore a deposition taken because the witness was about to go out of the Commonwealth, is admissible if the witness is out of the state at the time of the trial, although he testifies in the deposition that he has no present purpose of leaving the state.[2]

§ 221. After an action has been commenced by the service of process, or after it has been submitted

[1] R. L. ch. 175, § 26.

[2] Livesey *v.* Bennett, 14 Gray, 130.

to arbitrators or referees, either party may apply to a justice of the peace or special commissioner who shall issue a notice to the adverse party to appear before said justice or commissioner or any other justice of the peace or special commissioner at the time and place appointed for taking the deposition and propose interrogatories.[1]

§ 222. The brother-in-law of one who as stakeholder is made a party to a suit in equity, is not disqualified to take a deposition in the case as a justice of the peace. The stakeholder has no interest in the suit, for he was merely a trustee for both parties, and his brother-in-law, the justice of the peace who took the deposition, cannot be said therefore to be related to any party in interest in the suit.[2]

§ 223. The notice may be served on the adverse party, his agent or attorney; and if there are several plaintiffs or defendants, on any of them.[3]

§ 224. Where an attorney puts his name on the record as attorney to one of the parties in an action, notice given to him of the taking of a deposition will be sufficient, the party whom he represents being estopped by the record to allege that he appeared without authority.[4]

§ 225. The notice is to be served by delivering an attested copy thereof to the person to be noti-

[1] R. L. ch. 175, § 27.

[2] Culver *v.* Benedict, 13 Gray, 7.

[3] R. L. ch. 175, § 28.

[4] Smith *v.* Bowditch, 7 Pick. 137.

fied, or by leaving such copy at his place of abode, not less than twenty-four hours before the time appointed for taking the deposition, and also allowing not less time than at the rate of one day, Sundays excluded, for every twenty miles' travel to the place appointed.[1]

§ 226. The reading to the adverse party, by the officer serving it, of a notice of the time and place appointed for the taking of a deposition, is not a legal service of such notice.[2]

§ 227. The object of the statute is very clear. The person notified shall have not less than twenty-four hours' notice before the time required for his attendance; and if he has to travel to the place of attendance, he shall have sufficient time for that purpose, not less than at the rate of one day for every twenty miles' travel. The time and distance are measured by hours, and therefore fractions of a day may be computed, both as to notice and the time necessary to reach the place of appointment.[3]

§ 228. The general rule of law is, that every witness must give his evidence in person before the court and jury, so that they may be able to judge of his credibility by his appearance and manner of testifying. There are exceptions to this rule founded on considerations of convenience

[1] R. L. ch. 175, § 29.

[2] Young *v.* Capen, 7 Met. 287.

[3] Hubbard, J., in City Bank at Providence *v.* Fullerton, 11 Met. 73, at 78.

and necessity. But if a party desires to use the testimony of an absent witness, this can only be done by showing that the provisions of law regulating the mode of depositions have been complied with. If any essential requisite is omitted, the deposition, however full and accurate it may be in other respects, is not legal evidence. The intent of the statute was, in providing that the adverse party must have twenty-four hours' notice of the time for taking the deposition, that a party should not be suddenly called upon at the pleasure of his adversary to attend to the taking of material testimony, without having some time for preparation and to procure the attendance of counsel.[1]

Form of Notice to Adverse Parties.

COMMONWEALTH OF MASSACHUSETTS.

[Name of County] } ss.

To A. B., of B., in the county of M., *Greeting:*

Whereas C. D., of W., in the county of M. has requested me to take the deposition of E. F. of R., in the county of E., to be used in an action of [tort *or* contract] pending between you and the said C. D. and the [house, office, *or* store] of G. H. in said R., and the day of , in the year of our Lord one thousand nine hundred and , at of the clock in the noon, are appointed the time and place for the said deponent to testify what he know relating

[1] Bigelow, C. J., in Hunt *v.* Lowell Gas Light Co., 1 Allen, 343.

to said action. You are hereby notified that you may then and there be present, and put such interrogatories as you may think fit.

Given under my hand at , on the day of , in the year of our Lord one thousand nine hundred and .

S. P.,
Justice of the Peace.
[or *Special Commissioner.*]

§ 229. The justice or commissioner who takes the deposition may give a verbal instead of the written notice, or if the adverse party or his attorney in writing waives notice or if the defendant does not enter his appearance in the action within the time required by law, no notice is required.[1]

§ 230. The deponent must be sworn or affirmed to testify the truth, the whole truth and nothing but the truth, relative to the cause for which the deposition is taken. He is then examined by the justice or commissioner, and the parties if they think fit, and his testimony must be taken in writing.[2]

§ 231. The party producing the deponent shall be allowed first to examine him, either upon verbal or written interrogatories, on all the points which he considers material; the adverse party may then examine him in like manner; after which either party may propose further interrogatories.[3]

[1] R. L. ch. 175, § 30. [2] R. L. ch. 175, § 31.
[3] R. L. ch. 175, § 32.

§ 232. The deposition must be written by the justice, commissioner, deponent or by a disinterested person in the presence and under the direction of the justice or commissioner, must be carefully read to or by the deponent, and must then be subscribed by him.[1]

§ 233. A deposition which is certified as made and subscribed by the deponent is sufficient, for the meaning seems to be that the deposition was written either by the deponent himself, or by the justice or commissioner, or by some other person by the direction of the justice or commissioner; and that it was read to or by the deponent. For if it were not so written and read, it would seem that the justice or commissioner could not certify of his or her own knowledge that the deposition was made by the deponent.[2]

§ 234. Exhibits and documents annexed to a deposition are not required to be in the handwriting of the justice of the peace or special commissioner, or of some person appointed by him or her. Thus it is no objection to a deposition that the bill of items of the plaintiff's account annexed to the deposition, and sworn to by the deponent, is not in the handwriting of the justice of the peace or special commissioner who took the deposition, or of the deponent, or of some disinterested person.[3]

[1] R. L. ch. 175, § 33.

[2] Brown *v.* King, 5 Met. 173.

[3] Marvin *v.* Raigan, 12 Cush. 132.

§ 235. The justice or commissioner must annex to the deposition a certificate of the time and manner of taking it, the person at whose request, the cause in which it was taken, the reason for taking it, and that the adverse party attended, or if he did not attend what notice was given to him.[1]

§ 236. The testimony of witnesses in the form of depositions cannot be received, unless there has been a full compliance with the actual and positive requirements of the law. Therefore if the certificate of the justice or commissioner who took the deposition does not state that the deponent was sworn to tell the truth, the whole truth, and nothing but the truth, relating to the cause for which the deposition is taken, the law has not been complied with and the deposition will be of no effect.[2]

§ 237. It is the duty of the magistrate (justice of the peace or special commissioner) taking a deposition to state in his certificate "the reason for taking it;" but it is not necessary for the certificate to show in what manner or by what evidence he was satisfied of the existence of the cause for the taking. It is sufficient that he certifies to the fact upon his official responsibility.[3]

§ 238. If the certificate of a justice of the peace or special commissioner to a deposition shows that

[1] R. L. ch. 175, § 34.

[2] Simpson *v.* Carleton, 1 Allen, 109; Hitchings *v.* Ellis, 1 Allen, 475; Bacon *v.* Rogers, 8 Allen, 146.

[3] Littlehale *v.* Dix, 11 Cush. 364.

the deponent was sworn to testify in relation to an action pending between A. B. and C. D., it is sufficient, although it appears that another action with the same title is pending in the same court.[1]

§ 239. Where the deposition and the certificate are enclosed together, sealed up and directed to the clerk of the court by the justice of the peace, or special commissioner, the certificate is annexed to the deposition within the meaning of the statute. If not the best, it is one method of annexation.[2]

Certificate to be annexed to Deposition.

COMMONWEALTH OF MASSACHUSETTS.

[Name of County] } ss.

This is to certify that E. F., the above-named deponent, appeared before me at o'clock, M., on the day of , A. D. 190 , at [*state place*], and gave the foregoing deposition, to be used in an action of [tort *or* contract] now pending between A. B., of B., in the county of M., and C. D., of W., in the said county of M., before the Court for the county of ; that prior to his examination the said deponent was duly sworn by me to testify the truth, the whole truth, and nothing but the truth, relating to the cause for which said deposition is taken; that both parties to the said action had an opportunity to examine the said deponent as in the statute provided;

1 Hale *v.* Silloway, 3 Allen, 358.

2 Shaw *v.* McGregory, 105 Mass. 96.

that the said deposition was reduced to writing by me; that it was carefully read to the said deponent, and was then subscribed by him; that the said deposition was taken at the request of the [plaintiff *or* defendant] in said action, the said deponent being [*here state reason for taking the deposition*], and that the [plaintiff *or* defendant] in said action attended at the taking of said deposition [*if the adverse party did not attend, state the notice, if any, that was given him*].

Dated at this day of , A. D. 190 .

S. P.,
Justice of the Peace.
[or *Special Commissioner.*]

§ 240. The deposition must be delivered by the justice or commissioner to the court, arbitrators, referees or other persons before whom the cause is pending, or be enclosed and sealed by him or her and directed to it or them, and remains sealed until opened by it or them.[1]

§ 241. As the deposition with the annexed certificate is in the possession of the justice of the peace or special commissioner until it is transmitted by him or her, he or she may correct any error or supply by additional statements any deficiency discovered in the caption. But after it has been delivered to the court or tribunal where it is to be used, the deposition is in their custody, and no alteration, change or amendment in the certi-

[1] R. L. ch. 175, § 35.

ficate accompanying it can be made without their order or permission.[1]

SUMMONING OF WITNESSES.

§ 242. A person may be summoned and compelled to give his deposition at a place within twenty miles of his place of abode, in like manner and under the same penalties as are provided for a witness before a court.[2]

§ 243. A person not a resident of, but found within, this Commonwealth may be summoned and compelled to give his deposition at any place within ten miles of the place at which the summons is served upon him, in like manner and under the same penalties as he may be summoned and compelled to attend as a witness before a court.[3]

Form of Deposition Summons.

COMMONWEALTH OF MASSACHUSETTS.

[Name of County] } ss.

To E. F. of R., in the county of E., *Greeting:*

Whereas C. D. of W., in the county of M., has requested me to take your deposition, to be used in an action now pending between him and A. B. of B., in the

1 Hitchings *v.* Ellis, 1 Allen, 475.
2 R. L. ch. 175, § 40.
3 R. L. ch. 175, § 41.

county of M., and the [house, office, *or* store] of G. H. in said R., and the day of , in the year of our Lord one thousand nine hundred and at of the clock in the noon, are appointed the time and place for taking the same deposition.

You are hereby required, in the name of the Commonwealth of Massachusetts, then and there to appear, to testify what you know relating to the said action. Hereof fail not.

Given under my hand at aforesaid, the day of , in the year of our Lord one thousand nine hundred and .

S. T.,
Justice of the Peace.
[or *Special Commissioner.*]

§ 244. A person may be summoned and compelled, in like manner and under the same penalties as are provided for a witness before a court, to give his deposition in a cause pending in a court of any other state or government. Such deposition may be taken before a justice of the peace or special commissioner in this Commonwealth, or before a commissioner appointed under the authority of the state or government in which the action is pending. If the deposition is taken before such commissioner, the witness may be summoned and compelled to appear before him by process from a justice of the peace or special commissioner in this Commonwealth.[1]

[1] R. L. ch. 175, § 46.

DEPOSITIONS TO PERPETUATE TESTIMONY.

§ 245. If a person desires to perpetuate his own testimony or the testimony of another person he must apply in writing to two justices of the peace or special commissioners, one of whom must be an attorney at law, requesting them to take his deposition or the deposition of the person whose testimony he desires to perpetuate and stating briefly and substantially his title, claim or interest in or to the subject relative to which he desires the evidence perpetuated, the names of all other persons interested or supposed to be interested therein and the name of the witness proposed to be examined.[1]

§ 246. The justices or commissioners will thereupon cause notice of the time and place appointed for taking the deposition to be given to all persons named in said statement as interested in the case, in the manner provided in §§ 221, 223, 225, and 229, *ante;* and if in the opinion of the justices or commissioners no sufficient provision is made by law for giving notice to parties adversely interested, they will cause such reasonable notice to be given as they consider proper. A person may be summoned and compelled to give a deposition in perpetuation of his testimony in like manner and under the same penalties as are provided for a witness before a court.[2]

[1] R. L. ch. 175, § 47. [2] R. L. ch. 175, § 48.

§ 247. If at the time and place so appointed a witness or a person interested appears and objects, the justices are not to take the deposition unless upon hearing the parties they find that such testimony may be material to the petitioner and is not sought for the purpose of discovery or of using it in an action then pending or unless witness is the petitioner in an action thereafter to be brought against said witness, and that the petitioner is in danger of losing the same before it can be taken in any action wherein his right, title, interest or claim can be tried. In all cases the petitioner, his agent or attorney, is required, at the request of such witness or of a person interested, to be examined on oath relative to his reasons for taking the deposition.[1]

§ 248. The deponent must be sworn and examined, and his deposition be written, read and subscribed in the manner stated in §§ 230, 231, and 232, *ante;* and the justices must sign and annex thereto a certificate of the name of the person at whose request it was taken, the names of all persons who were notified to attend, of all who attended the taking thereof, of the time and manner of taking it, and that it was taken for the purpose of perpetuating the testimony therein.[2]

[1] R. L. ch. 175, § 49.

[2] R. L. ch. 175, § 50.

Form of Certificate to be annexed to Deposition to Perpetuate Testimony.

COMMONWEALTH OF MASSACHUSETTS.

[Name of County] } ss.
City [*or* town] of

This day of , in the year of our Lord one thousand nine hundred and , personally appeared before us the subscribers, two justices of the peace [*or* special commissioners] for the said Commonwealth, the aforesaid deponent, and after being carefully examined and duly cautioned to testify the truth, the whole truth, and nothing but the truth, made oath [*or* affirmed] that the foregoing deposition by him subscribed is true. Taken at the request of , to be preserved in perpetual remembrance of the thing. And we duly notified all persons living within twenty miles of this place of caption whom we knew to be interested in the property to which said deposition relates; and attended [*if any persons so notified did attend; or*, we not knowing any person living within twenty miles of said place of caption, interested in the property whereunto the said deposition relates, did not notify any persons to attend].

S. T., [Counsellor at law.]
U. V.,
Justices of the Peace.
[or *Special Commissioners.*]

§ 249. The deposition, the certificate and the application of the petitioner must, within ninety days after the taking of the deposition, be recorded in the registry of deeds in the county or district in which the land lies, if the deposition relates to land; otherwise in the county or district in which the parties or some of them reside.[1]

FEES.

§ 250. The statutory fees of justices of the peace for taking a deposition are fifty cents; for writing the deposition and caption, at the rate of twelve cents a page; for notice to the adverse party, twenty cents. The justice must certify his fees and the deponent's fees on the deposition. For taking a deposition to perpetuate testimony, each justice is entitled to the fees prescribed, for all services which are personally rendered by him.[2] The fees of special commissioners are the same as those of justices of the peace for like services.[3]

[1] R. L. ch. 175, § 51.
[2] R. L. ch. 204, § 1.
[3] R. L. ch. 17 § 5.

CHAPTER III.

CALLING OF MEETINGS.

CORPORATIONS.

§ 251. If, by reason of the death or absence of the officers of a corporation, or other cause, there is no person duly authorized to call or preside at a legal meeting, a justice of the peace may, upon a written application of three or more of the members, issue a warrant to any one of them, directing him to call a meeting by giving such notice as had been previously required by law, and may in the same warrant direct him to preside at the meeting until a clerk is duly chosen and qualified if no officer is present legally authorized to preside.[1]

§ 252. The justice of the peace who issues a warrant on the application of three persons representing themselves as members of a corporation, does not pass upon the question whether such persons are legal members of such corporation, or whether such meeting is, when assembled, a legal one, and competent to act on the business for which it is assembled.[2]

[1] R. L. ch. 109, § 15.

[2] Stevens *v.* Taft, 3 Gray, 487.

§ 253. A justice of the peace upon the written request of a majority of the acting directors of a corporation may call a special meeting of the stockholders to confirm the legality of the organization of the corporation or of any of its proceedings, whether the corporation is formed under the general corporation law or under a special statute.[1]

FIRE DISTRICTS.

§ 254. If the selectmen of a town, upon the application in writing of not less than seven freeholders, inhabitants of a proposed fire district, requiring them to notify a meeting of the voters of the district to consider the expediency of organizing such district and establishing a fire department, refuse or neglect to give notice of such meeting, a justice of the peace may do so. The justice must notify the meeting in the same manner that town meetings are notified.[2] (See § 263, *post.*)

GENERAL FIELDS.

§ 255. If several distinct lots or parcels of land are enclosed and fenced in one common field, or if all the proprietors of such lands agree so to enclose them, such enclosure is called a general field; and the proprietors, if not less than five in number,

[1] R. L. ch. 110, §§ 82, 83.
[2] R. L. ch. 32, § 51.

may from time to time, in manner as the Revised Laws provide, hold regular meetings for the purpose of managing their common concerns.[1]

§ 256. Upon the application of two or more proprietors of a general field to a justice of the peace, he will issue his warrant to one of the applicants, directing him to call a meeting of all the proprietors, and expressing in the warrant the time, place, occasion and purpose of the meeting.[2]

MEETING-HOUSE PROPRIETORS.

§ 257. A meeting of a corporation of proprietors of a meeting-house to alter, enlarge, repair, rebuild or remove its house, or to build a new one, may be called upon application in writing by any five of the members of the corporation, by a warrant issued by a justice of the peace, directed to one of the applicants.[3]

PRIVATE WAY AND BRIDGE PROPRIETORS.

§ 258. If four or more persons are the proprietors and rightful occupants of a private way or bridge, and three of them make application to a justice of the peace to call a proprietors' meeting, the justice may issue his warrant therefor, stating the time, place and purpose of the meeting. The

[1] R. L. ch. 123, § 18.
[2] R. L. ch. 123, § 19; cf. ibid., § 1 (see § 266, *post*).
[3] R. L. ch. 36, §§ 27, 29.

warrant must be posted in a public place of the town in which such way or bridge is situated, seven days at least before the time appointed for the meeting.[1]

PARISHES AND RELIGIOUS SOCIETIES.

§ 259. A justice of the peace may, upon the application of five or more members, call a meeting of a religious society which is legally capable of becoming a corporation, if there are no assessors or committee, or if such officers unreasonably refuse to call a meeting,[2] by issuing his warrant directed to some one of the applicants, stating the objects of the proposed meeting, and requiring him to warn the members of the society to meet at a time and place appointed in the warrant; and such warrant may be served by posting an attested copy thereof on the principal outer door of the meeting house of such society, or by leaving such copy with, or at the last and usual places of abode of, the members of the society seven days at least before such meeting; and, upon return thereof, the same or any other justice of the peace may preside at the meeting during the choice and qualification of a clerk and until a moderator is chosen; and the society may thereupon choose a moderator and do such other things as parishes may do at their

[1] R. L. ch. 51, § 25.
[2] R. L. ch. 36, § 11.

annual meetings, if the subject-matter thereof is inserted in the warrant.[1]

§ 260. Ten or more persons, male or female, who desire to form a religious society, may make an application therefor in writing to a justice of the peace. Such justice may thereupon issue his warrant in the manner set forth in the preceding section, directed to one of the applicants, stating the objects of the proposed society, and requiring him to warn said persons to meet at a time and place appointed in the warrant.[2]

TRUSTEES OF METHODIST EPISCOPAL CHURCHES.

§ 261. The first meeting of the trustees of any society of the Methodist Episcopal Church, or of the African Methodist Episcopal Church, may be called by a justice of the peace upon the application of three or more of the trustees. The provisions stated in the two preceding sections and in chapter 36 of the Revised Laws, in relation to the warning and organization of meetings of religious societies, so far as appropriate, apply to meetings for the organization of such trustees.[3]

SOCIAL LIBRARY CORPORATIONS.

§ 262. Upon application of five or more proprietors of a social library corporation organized

[1] R. L. ch. 36, § 22. [2] R. L. ch. 36, § 23.
[3] R. L. ch. 36, § 42.

under section twelve of chapter 40 of the Public Statutes, now obsolete, a justice of the peace may still, perhaps, issue his warrant to one of them, directing him to call a meeting of proprietors at the time and place and for the purpose expressed in the warrant.[1]

TOWN MEETINGS.

§ 263. If the selectmen of a town unreasonably refuse to call a town meeting, a justice of the peace, upon the application of ten or more voters of the town, may call a meeting by a warrant under his hand, stating the subjects to be acted upon, directed to the constables of the town if there are any; otherwise to any of the persons applying therefor, directing them to summon the inhabitants qualified to vote in town affairs, to assemble at the time and place, and for the purposes expressed in the warrant.[2] At every town meeting, except for the election of state officers, a moderator must first be chosen. Until the election of a moderator, the town clerk will preside, but if he is absent or if there is no town clerk, the chairman of the selectmen or the member longest in continuous service will preside, but if no selectman is present, the justice of the peace calling such meeting, if the meeting is so called, is to preside. Such presid-

[1] Pub. Sts. ch. 40, § 13; cf. R. L. ch. 38, § 1. See Rep. of Comrs. for Con. and Arr. Pub. Sts., ch. 38, notes.

[2] R. L. ch. 11, § 330.

ing officer will have the powers and perform the duties of a moderator.[1]

Application for a Town Meeting, when the Selectmen have declined to call one.

To S. T., Esq., a Justice of the Peace for the Commonwealth of Massachusetts:

The subscribers, residents in, and legal voters of, the town of M., in the county of P., show that application has been made to [*here state the names of the selectmen*], selectmen of said town, to call a meeting of the inhabitants thereof, duly qualified to vote at town meetings, [*here state the purpose for which it was sought to call the town meeting*].

But said selectmen have unreasonably refused to call a town meeting for those purposes. The said subscribers therefore request you to issue a warrant, as the law in such cases directs, for calling a meeting of said inhabitants for the purposes aforesaid.

Dated , 190 .

(Signed) [*by ten or more legal voters of the town*].

Warrant.

[Name of County] } ss.

To W. H., one of the constables [*or if there is no constable, then to one of the signers of the application*] of the town of M. in said county, *Greeting:*

Whereas A. B. and nine [*or more*] other residents in, and legal voters of, the said town, have represented to

1 R. L. ch. 11, § 331.

me the subscriber, a justice of the peace for the Commonwealth of Massachusetts, that application has been made to [*here state the names of the selectmen*], selectmen of said town, to call a meeting of the inhabitants of said town, qualified to vote in town meetings, [*here state the purpose for which it was sought to call the town meeting*], but they have unreasonably refused to call a meeting for those purposes; and said A. B. and said others have therefore made application to me to call one for those purposes.

These are therefore, in the name of the Commonwealth of Massachusetts, to require you to notify the inhabitants of said town, qualified by law to vote in town affairs, to assemble at , on , the day of next, at o'clock in the noon, for the purposes above mentioned.

Given under my hand this day of in the year of our Lord nineteen hundred and

S. T.,
Justice of the Peace.

WATCH DISTRICTS.

§ 264. Watch districts may be established and organized in villages containing not less than one thousand persons, for the protection of property against fire, thieves and robbers, and for keeping the streets quiet in the night-time.[1] A justice of the peace, in case of the refusal or neglect of the selectmen of the town, may, upon the application

[1] R. L. ch. 31, § 8.

in writing of not less than seven freeholders, inhabitants of such village, the limits of which must be defined in the application, requiring him to notify a meeting to consider the expediency of establishing such watch district, forthwith give notice to the voters in such district qualified to vote in town affairs, in the manner in which notice of town meetings is given, to assemble at some suitable place within the district for said purpose.[1] (See § 263, *ante.*)

§ 265. When a village in which a watch district may be established belongs to two or more towns, the voters thereof may organize such district at a meeting called and notified, as is stated in the preceding section, by a justice of the peace to whom application has been made by at least five voters of each town who are inhabitants of such district.[2]

PROPRIETORS OF WHARVES AND COMMON LANDS.

§ 266. Upon the written application of five or more proprietors of lands, wharves or other real estate held in common to a justice of the peace, stating that they intend to organize themselves as a corporation, he is required to issue his warrant to one of the applicants, directing him to call a meeting of all the proprietors and expressing in the warrant the time, place, occasion and purpose of the meeting.[3]

[1] R. L. ch. 31, § 9. [2] R. L. ch. 31, § 10.
[3] R. L. ch. 123, § 1.

CHAPTER IV.

ACKNOWLEDGMENT OF DEEDS.

IN GENERAL.

§ 267. The acknowledgment of a deed must be by the grantors or one of them, or by the attorney who executes the deed, and, if made in this Commonwealth, must be made before a justice of the peace, special commissioner or notary public; and the officer, before whom the acknowledgment is made, who should be a person not appearing on the face of the deed to be interested as one of the parties or otherwise,[1] must indorse upon or annex to the deed a certificate of such acknowledgment.[2]

§ 268. The only use of a certificate of the acknowledgment of a deed is to entitle the deed to be recorded. The certificate is not conclusive evidence that the grantor executed the deed.[3]

[1] Jones, Real Prop., §§ 1125, 1126.

[2] R. L. ch. 127, § 8; Acts of 1902, ch. 289.

[3] O'Neil *v.* Webster, 150 Mass. 572.

Forms of Acknowledgment of Deeds.

1. *Ordinary form.*

COMMONWEALTH OF MASSACHUSETTS.

Suffolk, ss. *Boston, March* 20, 1903.

Then personally appeared the above-named *Mary A. Brown* and acknowledged the foregoing instrument to be *her* free act and deed, before me,

S. T.
[*Justice of the Peace,*
Special Commissioner,
or *Notary Public.*]

2. *By two or more grantors.*

(*The caption used in the foregoing form is to be inserted in this and each of the following forms.*)

Then personally appeared the above-named *John Doe*, *Richard Rowe*, and *Noah Stowe*, and severally acknowledged the foregoing instrument to be their free act and deed, before me, etc.

3. *Where deed is executed by attorney.*

Then personally appeared the above named *Daniel Webster*, and acknowledged the foregoing instrument to be the free act and deed of the said *Samuel K. Norris*, before me, etc.

4. *Where a corporation is grantor.*

On this *first* day of *April*, 1901, before me appeared *Adam Gray*, to me personally known, who being by me duly sworn, [*or* affirmed] did say that he is the *Presi-*

dent of the *North American Lumber Corporation* and the seal affixed to said instrument is the corporate seal of the said corporation, and that said instrument was signed and sealed in behalf of said Corporation by authority of the *Board of Directors*, and said *Adam Gray* acknowledged said instrument to be the free act and deed of said corporation, before me, etc.

5. *Where a corporation is grantor.*
(*Shorter form.*)

Then personally appeared the above-named *Frank N. Stimpson* and acknowledged the foregoing instrument to be the free act and deed of the *Ajax Tack Company*, before me, etc.

§ 269. Justices of the peace in this Commonwealth may take acknowledgments of deeds conveying real estate situated outside of Massachusetts in many other states and territories. These states and territories are not enumerated here, as the authority to take such acknowledgments is purely statutory and hence liable to change. In most cases the authority of the justice, or the genuineness of his signature, must be authenticated in some way, usually by a clerk of a court of record under his seal. It is probable that special commissioners may act in such cases equally with justices of the peace.

OF SHARES OF STOCK.

§ 270. A justice of the peace or a special commissioner[1] may take acknowledgments of deeds of shares of stock which are sold by treasurers of corporations, because of the failure of the shareholders to pay the assessments due upon the shares.[2]

FEES.

§ 271. The statutory fee for taking the acknowledgment of a deed by one or more grantors, if taken at one time, is twenty-five cents.[3]

[1] R. L. ch. 17, § 5 (see § 205, *ante*).
[2] R. L. ch. 110, § 42.
[3] R. L. ch. 204, § 1.

CHAPTER V.

ISSUING OF WARRANTS.

IN CRIMINAL CASES.

(a) *Warrants.*[1]

§ 272. The office of justice of the peace is, as we have seen, of ancient origin. From the earliest times, until changed by recent legislation, it was one of the functions of justices of the peace to receive complaints and issue warrants for the apprehension of persons charged with crime. That power was taken away by Acts of 1877, ch. 211, and conferred upon certain other officers, to wit, trial justices and clerks of courts. It was found, however, to be inconvenient to require the inhabitants of a town in which neither a trial justice nor a clerk resided to go in search of such an officer in order to make complaint. To remedy this difficulty, Acts of 1879, ch. 254, of which Acts of 1884, ch. 286, and Acts of 1897, ch. 461, are amendments, was enacted, and the right to receive complaints

[1] Forms for warrants of various kinds may be had at the clerk's office of the district or police court in the district of which the justice of the peace is commissioned to issue warrants and take bail.

and issue warrants was restored to such justices of the peace as might be appointed by the governor. It seems that justices who are thus vested with special powers, are not holding a plurality of offices in violation of the Massachusetts Constitution, Ch. VI., Art II.[1]

§ 273. Having thus traced the legislation relating to *Warrants*, we may intelligently examine the present statute. It provides that the governor, with the advice and consent of the council, may from time to time, upon the petition of the mayor and aldermen of a city or the selectmen of a town which is included within the judicial district of a police or district court, and in which neither a justice nor the clerk of such court resides, designate and commission a justice of the peace who resides in said city or town to issue warrants returnable to said court and to take bail in criminal cases arising within such judicial district.[2] The fee for issuing such a warrant is one dollar.[3]

§ 274. The governor, with the advice and consent of the council, may from time to time designate and commission a justice of the peace who resides in the city of Quincy to issue warrants returnable to the district court of East Norfolk and to take bail in criminal cases arising within the judicial district of said court.[4]

[1] 1 Opinions Attys-Gen., 318.

[2] R. L. ch. 161, § 3.

[3] R. L. ch. 204, § 1.

[4] R. L. ch. 161, § 4.

§ 275. A justice of the peace who has been designated and commissioned, as is stated in the two preceding sections, with authority to issue warrants in criminal cases, may lawfully receive the complaints upon which such warrants are issued. Since the warrants cannot be issued without complaints, authority to receive complaints is implied from the authority to issue warrants.[1]

§ 276. A justice of the peace who has authority to issue warrants in criminal cases arising anywhere within a certain district, and whose residence falls within a new town formed by the incorporation of a part of an old town in the district, may continue to issue warrants in cases which arise within the new town, as well as elsewhere in the district.[2]

§ 277. A justice of the peace has no authority to direct his warrant to a private person, except where it is absolutely necessary, and where the necessity is expressed in the warrant; but he must direct it to a sheriff, deputy sheriff or constable.[3]

§ 278. Upon complaint made to the justice of the peace that a crime has been committed, he must examine the complainant and any witnesses produced by him, under oath, reduce the complaint to writing and cause it to be subscribed by the

[1] Commonwealth *v.* Taber, 155 Mass. 5; Commonwealth *v.* O'Hanlon, ibid., 198.

[2] Commonwealth *v.* Brennan, 150 Mass. 63.

[3] Commonwealth *v.* Foster, 1 Mass. 488.

complainant, and, if it appears that a crime has been committed, he will, except as provided in Revised Laws, chapter 217, §§ 23 to 27, inclusive, issue a warrant, reciting the substance of the accusation and requiring the officer to whom it is directed forthwith to arrest the accused and to take him before a court or trial justice of the county, to be dealt with according to law, and to summon such witnesses as shall be therein named to appear and give evidence on the examination.[1]

§ 279. A justice of the peace who is not designated and commissioned as a trial justice has no power, authority or jurisdiction to try cases, civil or criminal, receive complaints or issue warrants, except as provided in sections three and four of chapter 161 of the Revised Laws (see §§ 273, 274, *ante*); but a justice of the peace who is also a clerk or assistant clerk of a police, district or municipal court may receive complaints and issue warrants, returnable before the police, district or municipal court or trial justice which has jurisdiction of the trial or examination of the person charged with the offence.[2]

(*b*) *Bail.*

§ 280. In cases where the offence charged in the warrant is not punishable by death or im-

[1] R. L. ch. 217, § 22.
[2] R. L. ch. 161, § 5.

prisonment in the state prison, the justice may admit the person arrested to bail by taking from him a recognizance with sufficient sureties for his appearance in the court within the judicial district of which the offence charged was committed.[1]

§ 281. The justice of the peace who so admits the defendant to bail must certify that fact upon the warrant, and deliver it with the recognizance to the officer.[2]

IN OTHER CASES.

(*a*) *Entry by Board of Health.*

§ 282. If the board of health considers it necessary for the preservation of life or health to enter any land, building or premises, or go on board a vessel within its town, for the purpose of examining into and destroying, removing or preventing a nuisance, source of filth or cause of sickness, and the board, or any agent thereof sent for that purpose, is refused such entry, any member of the board or such agent may make complaint to a justice of the peace authorized to issue warrants in criminal cases, who may thereupon issue a warrant, directed to the sheriff or any of his deputies, to such member or agent of the board, or to any constable of such town, commanding him to take sufficient aid, and at any reasonable time repair to the place where such nuisance, source of

[1] R. L. ch. 217, § 29. [2] R. L. ch. 217, § 30.

filth or cause of sickness complained of may be, and to destroy, remove or prevent the same, under the directions of the board.[1]

Form of the Warrant.

COMMONWEALTH OF MASSACHUSETTS.

[Name of County] } ss.

To the Sheriff of our County of S., or any of his deputies, or any Constable of the city [*or* town] of B., or to T., agent of the Board of Health of the said city [*or* town] within our said county, *Greeting:*

Whereas complaint under oath [*or* affirmation] is made to me, the subscriber, a justice of the peace for the said Commonwealth, authorized to issue warrants in criminal cases therein, by , [a member *or* agent, *as the case may be*] of the board of health of the said city [*or* town] of B., that of the said city [*or* town] of B. has caused to exist a [nuisance, cause of sickness, *or* source of filth, *as the case may be*], [*here particularly describe the nuisance and state its locality*], and the same nuisance does still keep up and continue. You are therefore, in behalf of said Commonwealth, commanded to take sufficient aid, and at any reasonable time to repair to said place where said [nuisance, source of filth *or* cause of sickness] exists, and to destroy, remove or prevent the same, under the directions of said board of health.

[1] R. L. ch. 75, § 74.

Given under my hand this day of , in the year of our Lord nineteen hundred and .

S. T.,
Justice of the Peace.

(*b*) *Entry of Premises of Gas Consumer.*

§ 283. An officer or servant of a gas-light company, who is duly authorized in writing by the president, treasurer, agent or secretary of said company, may at any reasonable time enter any premises which are supplied with gas by such company for the purpose of examining or removing the meters, pipes, fittings and works for supplying or regulating the supply of gas and of ascertaining the quantity of gas consumed or supplied; and if any person, directly or indirectly, prevents or hinders such officer or servant from so entering such premises or from making such examination or removal, such officer or servant may make complaint to a justice of the peace authorized to issue criminal process who may thereupon issue a warrant directed to the sheriff or to either of his deputies, or to a constable of the city or town in which such company is located, commanding him to take sufficient aid and repair to said premises accompanied by such officer or servant, who may examine such meters, pipes, fittings and works for supplying or regulating the supply of gas, and ascertain the quantity of gas consumed or supplied therein, and, if required, remove any meters, pipes, fittings and works belonging to said company.[1]

Form of the Warrant.

COMMONWEALTH OF MASSACHUSETTS.

[Name of County] } ss.

To the Sheriff of the County of S., or any of his deputies, or any Constable of the city [*or* town] of B., within our said county, *Greeting:*

Whereas complaint under oath [*or* affirmation] is made to me, the subscriber, a justice of the peace for the said Commonwealth, authorized to issue criminal process, by T., an officer [*or* servant, *as the case may be*] of the C. Company, a corporation organized for the purpose of supplying gas to the inhabitants of the said city [*or* town] of B., said T. being duly authorized, in writing, by the [president, treasurer, agent *or* secretary] of the said company, that he has been prevented from entering the premises of D., situated in said city [*or* town] of B. [*here describe premises and state locality*], for the purpose of [*here state purpose for which entry to the premise was sought*]. You are therefore, in behalf of the Commonwealth, commanded to take sufficient aid and to repair to said premises with said T., and cause him to enter for the purpose aforesaid.

[1] R. L. ch. 58, § 15.

Given under my hand, this day of , in the year of our Lord nineteen hundred and .

S. T.,
Justice of the Peace.

(*c*) *Search for Liquor illegally kept.*

§ 284. If two persons of full age make complaint to a justice of the peace authorized to issue warrants in criminal cases, that they have reason to believe and do believe that spirituous or intoxicating liquor, described in the complaint, is kept or deposited by a person named therein in a store, shop, warehouse, building, vehicle, steamboat, vessel or place, and is intended for sale contrary to law, or has been brought into a city or town in violation of the provisions of sections 48, 49 and 51 of chapter 100 of the Revised Laws, such justice of the peace, if it appears that there is probable cause to believe said complaint to be true, is required to issue a search warrant to a sheriff, deputy sheriff, city marshal, chief of police, deputy chief of police, deputy marshal, police officer or constable, commanding him to search the premises in which it is alleged that such liquor is deposited, and to seize such liquor, the vessels in which it is contained and all implements of sale and furniture used or kept and provided to be used in the illegal keeping or sale of such liquor, and securely keep the same until final action thereon, and return the warrant with his doings thereon, as soon as may be, to a court or trial justice having jurisdiction in the place in which such liquor is alleged to be kept or deposited.[1]

Form of Complaint to search for Intoxicating Liquor.

COMMONWEALTH OF MASSACHUSETTS.

[Name of County] } ss.

To N. C., Esquire, a justice of the peace, authorized to issue warrants in criminal cases in the town of B., in the county of M.

J. S. and L. P., both of said B., and both being of full age, in behalf of the Commonwealth of Massachusetts on oath complain that they have reason to believe, and do believe, that intoxicating liquors, to wit, [*here describe the liquors as* a certain quantity of rum, being about, and not exceeding gallons; a certain quantity of gin, etc., *according to the facts*] on the day of , in the year nineteen hundred and , were and still are kept and deposited by D. E., of said B., in a certain , situate [*here describe the building or other place, with particulars of its location sufficient to identify it*] in said B., and occupied by said D. E., and which liquors were intended by said D. E. for sale in this Commonwealth, contrary to law, said D. E. not being authorized to sell the same in this Commonwealth, or keep the same

[1] R. L. ch. 100, § 72.

for sale, for any purpose, by any legal authority whatever, against the peace of the Commonwealth and the form of the statute in such case made and provided; and said complainants pray for a warrant to search said , described as aforesaid for liquors, and that the same may be declared to be forfeited, and that said D. E. and all other persons claiming an interest in said liquors may be summoned to appear before a court having jurisdiction of the case, to show cause, if any they have, why said liquors should not be declared forfeited. [*If the place intended to be searched is a dwelling-house, and no tavern, store, grocery, eating-room or place of common resort is kept therein, the complaint should conclude as follows:* —] [1]

(And I, J. S., one of the above complainants, on oath, say that I have reason to believe, and do believe, that intoxicating liquor, such as above mentioned, has been sold in the house above mentioned [*or* has been taken from the house above mentioned for the purpose of being sold,] by the occupant of said house, or with the consent and permission of the occupant of said house, contrary to law, within one month next before this day, and that said liquor above mentioned is now kept in said house for sale by D. E., contrary to law, and my belief aforesaid is founded on the following facts and circumstances: [*here let such facts and circumstances be stated*].)

J. S.
L. P.

Received and sworn to at said B., before me this day of , in the year nineteen hundred and

[1] R. L. ch. 100, § 73.

and it appears to me that there is probable cause to believe the foregoing complaint to be true.

N. C.,
Justice of the Peace.

Form of Warrant to Search for and Seize Liquors unlawfully kept for Sale.

COMMONWEALTH OF MASSACHUSETTS.

[Name of County] } ss.

To the Sheriff of our county of M., or either of his deputies, or any Constable of the town of B., in said county, *Greeting:*

Whereas J. S. and L. P., both of said B., and both of full age, on the day of , in the year nineteen hundred and , at said B., in behalf of the Commonwealth aforesaid, on oath complained to the undersigned, a justice of the peace authorized to issue warrants in criminal cases in said town of B., that they have reason to believe, and do believe, that on the day of , in the year nineteen hundred and , at said B., intoxicating liquors, to wit, [*here describe the liquors as in the complaint*] are kept and deposited by D. E. of said B., in a certain , situate [*here describe the building or other place, as in the complaint*] in said B., and occupied by said D. E. as a , and that said liquors were, and are, intended for sale by the said D. E., in this Commonwealth, contrary to law, he, said D. E., not being then and there authorized to sell or keep such liquors for sale in this Commonwealth for any purpose by any legal authority whatever; whereby said liquors have become forfeited. [*In case the place to be searched is a dwelling-house, and no tavern, store, grocery, eating-room or place of common resort is kept therein, the warrant should contain the following clause. But in a warrant for searching any other place besides a dwelling-house, the following clause should be omitted.*]

(And J. S., one of the said complainants, has duly made oath that he has reason to believe, and doth believe, that intoxicating liquors, such as are mentioned in the complaint, have been sold in said house, by the occupant thereof, or with the permission and consent of the occupant thereof, [*or* have been taken from said house for the purpose of being sold,] contrary to law, within one month next before making the complaint, and that such liquors are kept and deposited in said house, by said D. E., and intended for sale in this Commonwealth, contrary to law, and has, in his said oath, stated the following facts and circumstances on which his said belief was founded: [*here let the facts and circumstances be repeated, as in the complaint*].)

And said complainants have also prayed that due process may issue to search for said liquors, and that such further proceeding may be had in the premises as to law and justice in that behalf may appertain ; and whereas it appears to me, the subscriber, on the complaint aforesaid, that probable cause has been shown for the issuing of a warrant of search thereupon:

These, therefore, are to require you, in the name of the Commonwealth, taking with you proper assistants, forthwith to enter the herein above described, and make diligent and careful search for all the liquors herein above described, and if such liquors are found therein, to seize and convey the same, and the vessels which contain such liquors, and all implements of sale or furniture used, or kept and provided to be used, in the illegal keeping or sale of such liquors, to some place of safety, and safely keep the same, to await the final action and decision of the court upon said complaint.

Herein fail not, and make due return of this warrant, with your doings thereon, to the Court of .

Witness my hand at said B., this day of , in the year nineteen hundred and .

N. C.,
Justice of the Peace.

(*d*) *Impounding Beasts.*

§ 285. If the owner or keeper of beasts which have been impounded is dissatisfied with the claim of the person impounding them, he may have the amount for which he is liable determined by two disinterested persons, to be appointed and sworn by a justice of the peace.[1]

FORMS.

Warrant for ascertaining Damage done by Beasts taken up and Impounded, to be issued at the request of the Owners of such Beasts.

To A. B. and C. D. of , two disinterested and judicious persons, *Greeting:*

You are hereby appointed and empowered faithfully and impartially to estimate upon oath the damage done

[1] R. L. ch. 33, § 33.

to E. F. by [*here describe the beasts*], which for that cause have been taken up by G. H. and impounded [*here state the pound and place where impounded*].

Given under my hand this day of , in the year of our Lord nineteen hundred and .

S. T.,
Justice of the Peace.

Oath.

[Name of County] } ss.

The above [*or* within] named A. B. and C. D. personally appeared and made oath that in estimating the above [*or* within] mentioned damages, they would act faithfully and impartially, according to their best skill and judgment.

Before me, S. T.,
Justice of the Peace.

Appraisers' Return.

B. , 190 .

Pursuant to the within warrant, we have considered the damage done by the beasts within mentioned, and do upon oath estimate the same at .

A. B.
C. D.

§ 286. A justice of the peace, upon application from the person who has impounded beasts and who has not received the sum for which the beasts were impounded within fourteen days after notice of the impounding was given as directed in section 32 of chapter 33 of the Revised Laws, or after the last publication of such notice, is required to issue a warrant to two disinterested persons to be appointed and sworn by such justice, directing them to determine the sum due from the owner or keeper of the beasts.[1]

FORMS.

Warrant for Estimating the Damage done by Beasts taken up and Impounded, to be issued on the application of the one who Impounded them.

To A. B. and C. D. of , two disinterested and judicious persons, *Greeting:*

You are hereby appointed and empowered faithfully and impartially to estimate upon oath the damage done to E. F. by [*here describe the beasts*], which for that cause have been taken up and impounded by G. H. [*in such pound or in such place*], and also in like manner to appraise so many of the said beasts as shall be sufficient to answer the said damages and all charges.

Given under my hand this day of , in the year of our Lord nineteen hundred and .

S. T.,
Justice of the Peace.

Oath.

[Name of County] } ss.

The above [*or* within] named A. B. and C. D. personally appeared and made oath, that in estimating the

[1] R. L. ch. 33, § 34.

within [*or* above] mentioned damages and appraising any of the within mentioned beasts, they would act faithfully and impartially, according to their best skill and judgment.

Before me, S. T.,
Justice of the Peace.

Appraisers' Return.

Pursuant to the within warrant, we have considered the damage done by the beasts within mentioned, and do upon oath estimate the same at .

We have also appraised the following beasts [*or* the said beasts] to answer said damages [*here insert the kind and price*].

A. B.
C. D.

(*e*) *Infected Articles.*

§ 287. If, upon application of the board of health of a town, it appears to a justice of the peace authorized to issue warrants, that there is just cause to suspect that baggage, clothing or goods, found within the town, are infected with any disease dangerous to the public health, he must, by warrant directed to the sheriff or his deputy or to any constable, require him to impress as many men as said justice may judge necessary to secure such baggage, clothing or goods, and to post said men as a guard over the house or place containing such articles to prevent persons from removing or coming near the same until due inquiry is made into the circumstances.[1]

[1] R. L. ch. 75, § 87.

§ 288. The justice may, by the same warrant, require the officers, under the direction of the board, to impress and take up convenient houses or stores for the safe keeping of such articles.[1]

FORM

of the Warrant.

[Name of County] } ss.

To the Sheriff of our county of S., or any of his deputies, or any Constable of the city [*or* town] of B., within our said county, *Greeting:*

It appearing to me the subscriber, a justice of the peace for the Commonwealth of Massachusetts, authorized to issue warrants, upon application of the board of health of said town, that there is just cause to suspect that [baggage, clothing *or* goods] at , within said town, are infected with [*here state the disease*] dangerous to the public health. You are hereby directed, in the name of the said Commonwealth, to impress [*here state the number*] men and secure said [baggage, clothing *or* goods], and to post said men as a guard over [*here state the place where the articles are*], and to take up, under the direction of said board of health, such houses or stores as may be convenient for the keeping of said articles.

Given under my hand this day of , in the year of our Lord nineteen hundred and .

S. T.,

Justice of the Peace.

[1] R. L. ch. 75, § 88.

(*f*) *Lost Goods, Appraisals.*

§ 289. A justice of the peace, upon application of a finder of lost goods or stray beasts of the value of ten dollars or more, is required to issue a warrant directed to two disinterested persons, to be appointed by such justice, and returnable into the office of the clerk of the city or town where said property was found within seven days from the date, requiring them to appraise the lost goods or stray beasts at their true value, upon oath which may be administered by the justice.[1]

FORM.

Warrant to appraise Lost Goods or Stray Beasts.

To A. B. of , and C. D. of , two disinterested and judicious persons, *Greeting:*

By virtue of the power and authority to me given, in and by section three of chapter ninety-four of the Revised Laws, I do hereby appoint you to appraise upon oath, at the true value thereof in money, according to your best skill and judgment, [*here mention the goods or beasts found*] found by E. F. within the city [*or* town] of G., in the county of M. , and of the value of ten dollars or more. Having performed this service, you are to make return of this warrant into the clerk's office of said G. within seven days from the date hereof.

[1] R. L. ch. 94, § 3.

Given under my hand this day of in the year of our Lord nineteen hundred and

S. T.,
Justice of the Peace.

Oath.

[Name of County] } ss. 190 .

The above-named A. B. and C. D. personally appeared and made oath, that they would faithfully and impartially perform the service to which they are appointed by the above warrant.

Before me, S. T.,
Justice of the Peace.

§ 290. Special commissioners have like powers as justices of the peace to appoint appraisers in all cases.[1]

§ 291. The statute provides that, in case of disagreement between the owner and the finder of lost money, goods or beasts, as to what are the proper charges for the former to pay to the latter, a justice of the peace shall determine the amount of the charges.[2]

(*g*) *Removal of Sick Persons.*

§ 292. A justice of the peace authorized to issue warrants in criminal cases may issue a warrant

[1] R. L. ch. 17, § 5. [2] R. L. ch. 94, § 4.

directed to the sheriff of the county or his deputy, or to any constable or police officer, requiring them under the direction of the board to remove any person who is infected with contagious disease, or to impress and take up convenient houses, lodging, nurses, attendants and other necessaries.[1]

FORM

of the Warrant.

[Name of County] } ss.

To the Sheriff of our county of S., or any of his deputies, or any Constable of the city [*or* town] of B., within our said county, *Greeting:*

Whereas complaint is made to me, the subscriber, a justice of the peace for the Commonwealth of Massachusetts, authorized to issue warrants in criminal cases, by the board of health of said city [*or* town] of B., that are [*or* is] sick with , at the house of , in said town, and ought to be removed therefrom for the safety of the public health. You are hereby required, in the name of the Commonwealth of Massachusetts, with the advice and under the direction of the board of health of the said city [*or* town] of B., to remove from the house of , in said city [*or* town] to [*or* to impress, *here state the articles which are judged* necessary for the accommodation, *or* safety and relief, of the said , *as the case may be*].

1 R. L. ch. 75, § 46.

Given under my hand this day of in the year of our Lord nineteen hundred and

S. T.,
Justice of the Peace.

(*h*) *Fees.*

§ 293. The statutory fee for granting a warrant of appraisal is twenty cents.[1]

[1] R. L. ch. 204, § 1.

CHAPTER VI.

OATHS AND AFFIDAVITS.

IN GENERAL.

§ 294. Justices of the peace and special commissioners may administer oaths or affirmations in all cases in which an oath is required, unless otherwise expressly provided.[1]

§ 295. The usual mode of administering oaths now practised in this Commonwealth, with the ceremony of holding up the hand, must be observed in all cases in which an oath may be administered by law,[2] except as otherwise provided in Revised Laws, chapter 175, §§ 16 to 19 inclusive.

NOMINATION PAPER AFFIDAVITS.

§ 296. A justice of the peace or special commissioner, when taking the oath of a signer of a nomination paper, as provided in section 144 of chapter 11 of the Revised Laws, must be satisfied that the person to whom the oath is administered is the person signing such nomination paper, and must so state in the attestation of said oath, under pen-

[1] R. L. ch. 161, § 2. [2] R. L. ch. 175, § 15.

alty of a fine of not less than ten or more than fifty dollars.[1]

FORECLOSURE AFFIDAVITS.

§ 297. The certificate of an entry made for the purpose of foreclosing a mortgage for breach of condition thereof may be sworn to before a justice of the peace or special commissioner.[2]

§ 298. A certificate of the entry of a mortgagee, for the purpose of foreclosure, sworn to before himself as a justice of the peace, is invalid. It is as contrary to elementary principles of justice to allow a magistrate to administer the requisite oath to such a certificate of his own entry under a mortgage to himself, as to permit him to take in his official capacity a deposition in a suit to which he is a party, or an acknowledgment of a deed to himself, or a recognizance for a debt due to him personally.[3]

NOTARIES PUBLIC AND BANK OFFICERS.

§ 299. Justices of the peace or special commissioners may receive the oaths of notaries' public and bank officers that the statements which they have made concerning the contents of boxes or safes in safety deposit vaults which have been opened for non-payment of rent, are true; and must

1 R. L. ch. 11, §§ 145, 397.

2 R. L. ch. 187, § 2.

3 Judd *v.* Tryon, 131 Mass. 345.

make a certificate thereof in a book kept by the corporation for recording the proceedings of the notary who opens and removes the contents of the box or safe.[1]

OFFICERS OF RELIGIOUS SOCIETIES.

§ 300. A justice of the peace or a special commissioner may administer the oaths of office to the clerks, assessors, treasurers and collectors of religious societies.[2]

PEDLERS.

§ 301. Justices of the peace and special commissioners may certify the oaths of pedlers that they are the persons named in their certificates, and that they are, or have declared their intention to become, citizens of the United States.[3]

RAILROAD POLICE.

§ 302. Railroad and steamboat police officers may be sworn before a justice of the peace or a special commissioner.[4]

RETURN OF CERTIFICATE OF OATH.

§ 303. A justice of the peace who administers the oath of office to any town officer is required,

[1] R. L. ch. 116, § 38; cf. ch. 17, § 5 (see § 205, *ante*).
[2] R. L. ch. 36, § 14; cf. ch. 17, § 5 (see § 205, *ante*).
[3] R. L. ch. 65, § 19; cf. ch. 17, § 5 (see § 205, *ante*).
[4] R. L. ch. 108, § 15; cf. ch. 17, § 5 (see § 205, *ante*).

within seven days thereafter, to return to the town clerk a certificate of the administering of such oath.[1]

FEES.

§ 304. The statutory fee of a justice of the peace for administering an oath required by law, except on a trial or examination before him, to one or more persons at one time, and of a special commissioner for the same act, is twenty-five cents.[2]

[1] R. L. ch. 25, § 61.

[2] R. L. ch. 204, § 1 ; cf. ch. 17, § 5 (see § 205, *ante*).

CHAPTER VII.

GENERAL POWERS AND DUTIES.

APPOINTMENT OF APPRAISERS.

§ 305. A disinterested justice of the peace or special commissioner may appoint appraisers of any part of the estate of a deceased person which may be in the county in which such justice or commissioner resides. The appraisers must be suitable, disinterested persons, three in number, and be sworn to the faithful performance of their duties. The justice of the peace or special commissioner who appoints them will issue an order to them, in substance as follows: —

[Name of County] } ss.

To , of in said county. You are hereby appointed to appraise on oath the estate and effects of , late of , deceased which may be in said county. When you have performed that service, you will deliver this order and your doings in pursuance thereof to , executor [*or* administrator, *as the case may be*] of said deceased, that he may return the same to the probate court for the county of .

Given under my hand this day of , in the year .

....

Justice of the Peace.[1]
[or *Special Commissioner.*]

[1] R. L. ch. 139, §§ 6, 7; cf. ch. 17, § 5 (see § 205, *ante*).

§ 306. The statutory fee of a justice of the peace or special commissioner for granting a warrant of appraisal is twenty cents.[1]

ARBITRATION.

§ 307. Controversies which might be the subject of a personal action at law or of a suit in equity may be submitted to the decision of one or more arbitrators in the following manner:[2] —

The parties must appear in person or by their lawful agents or attorneys before a justice of the peace or special commissioner and there sign and acknowledge an agreement in substance as follows: —

Know all men that , of , and , of , hereby agree to submit the demand, a statement whereof is hereto annexed [and all other demands between them, *as the case may be*], to the determination of and , the award of whom, or of a majority of whom, being made and reported within one year from this day to the superior court for the county of , the judgment thereon shall be final; and if either of the parties neglects to appear before the arbitrators, after due notice given to him of the time and place appointed for hearing the parties, the arbitrators may proceed in his absence.

Dated this day of , in the year

....

....

[1] R. L. ch. 204, § 1; cf. ch. 17, § 5 (see § 205, *ante*).

[2] R. L. ch. 194, § 1.

The justice or special commissioner, either of whom may be one of the arbitrators, will annex to the agreement a certificate, in substance as follows: —

[Name of County] } ss. 190 .

Then the above-named and personally appeared [*or* the above-named personally, and said by , his attorney, appeared, *as the case may be*], and acknowledged the above instrument by them signed to be their free act; before me,

....

Justice of the Peace.
[or *Special Commissioner.*] [1]

§ 308. The statutory fees of the justice or special commissioner in a reference to arbitration, for the agreement of submission and acknowledgment, are forty cents.[2]

§ 309. A submission to arbitration to which a partnership is one party, must show who are members of the firm,[3] and when a submission to arbitration entered into before a justice of the peace, or special commissioner is signed by several partners on the one part, it must be acknowledged by all of the partners who signed it.[4]

1 R. L. ch. 194, § 2.

2 R. L. ch. 194, § 13.

3 Wesson *v.* Newton, 10 Cush. 114.

4 Abbott *v.* Dexter, 6 Cush. 108; Horton *v.* Wilde, 8 Gray, 425.

ARREST ON MESNE PROCESS.

§ 310. A justice of the peace, except in the county of Suffolk, may receive the affidavit required of, or in behalf of, a plaintiff who is seeking to arrest a person on mesne process in an action of contract. The plaintiff, or the person in his behalf, must make affidavit, and prove to the satisfaction of the justice of the peace, the following statements: —

First, That he has good cause of action and reasonable expectation of recovering a sum amounting to twenty dollars exclusive of all costs which have accrued in any former action;

Second, That he believes and has reason to believe that the defendant has property, not exempt from being taken on execution, which he does not intend to apply to the payment of the plaintiff's claim; and,

Third, That he believes and has reason to believe that the defendant intends to leave the Commonwealth, so that execution, if obtained, cannot be served upon him;

Or, instead of the second and third, that the defendant is an attorney at law, or a person, member of a firm, agency or association engaged in the business of collecting money, that the debt sought to be recovered is for money collected by the defendant for the plaintiff and that the defendant unreasonably neglects to pay the same to the plaintiff.

Such affidavit and the certificate of the justice of the peace that he is satisfied it is true, must be annexed to the writ.[1]

§ 311. A justice of the peace, except in the county of Suffolk, may receive the affidavit required of, or on behalf of, a plaintiff who is seeking to arrest a person on mesne process in an action of tort, that he believes and has reason to believe that he has a good cause of action against the defendant, that he has reasonable expectation of recovering an amount equal, at least, to one third of the damages claimed in the writ, and that he believes and has reason to believe that the defendant intends to leave the Commonwealth, so that execution, if obtained, cannot be served upon him; and such affidavit, with a certificate of the justice of the peace that he is satisfied it is true, must be annexed to the writ.[2]

§ 312. The fees of the justice of the peace for hearing an application for a certificate to arrest on mesne process in actions of tort or of contract, are one dollar, to be paid in advance.[3]

[1] R. L. ch. 168, § 1.

[2] R. L. ch. 168, § 2. Query: Whether a special commissioner, by virtue of R. L. ch. 17, § 5, may take the affidavits described in these two sections. The magistrate is required to do more than simply take an affidavit; he must also pass upon its truth.

[3] R. L. ch. 168, § 75.

POWERS AND LIABILITIES AS CONSERVATORS OF THE PEACE.

§ 313. While the powers and duties of justices of the peace, particularly as conservators of the peace, have been conferred by statute, yet these statutes date so far back in the history of English law, that they may be said to be common law powers, which were adopted by us in the United States from the English law, together with the office of justice of the peace, and to be inseparable from the office, like the powers and duties of a sheriff.[1]

§ 314. It is further provided by statute in Massachusetts that "Justices of the peace shall be conservators of the peace throughout the Commonwealth and as such *may*, upon view of an affray, riot, assault or battery, without a warrant in writing, command the assistance of every sheriff, deputy sheriff, constable and police officer and of all other persons present for its suppression and for the arrest of all persons concerned therein as provided in chapters two hundred and sixteen and two hundred and seventeen of the Revised Laws. Persons so arrested shall be taken before a police, district or municipal court or a trial justice for examination." [2]

§ 315. The liability, if any, of a justice of the

[1] People *ex rel.* Burby *v.* Howland and Others, 55 Albany L. J. 319.

[2] R. L. ch. 166, § 2.

peace for failure to act as peace warden when a breach of the peace is committed in his presence is not, however, defined by this statute. The statute simply says that he *may* act. But since, where a statute directs the doing of a thing for the sake of justice or the public good, the word "may is the same as the word 'shall,'" it is submitted that a legal obligation is cast upon the peace officer to act.[1] Clearly he is not liable *civiliter*;[2] "no man ever heard of an action brought against a conservator [of the peace] as such."[3] But it is submitted that he is liable *criminaliter*, for "it is an undisputed principle of the common law, that for a breach of a public duty, an officer is punishable by indictment."[4]

Thus, (*hypothetical*) X, a deputy sheriff, was summoned by citizens to quell a disturbance at a public gathering in a country village some miles away, and refused to act without a warrant, knowing none was immediately obtainable. Y, a justice of the peace, present at the disturbance, also failed to act. It would seem that both are liable *criminaliter*.[5]

§ 316. If a prisoner, lawfully arrested without a warrant by order of a justice of the peace, for

[1] Rex et Regina *v.* Barlow, 2 Salk. 609.

[2] South *et al.* *v.* State of Maryland, Use of Pottle, 18 How. 396.

[3] *Per Lord Camden*, J., Entick *v.* Carrington, State Trials, vol. 19, page 1061.

[4] South *et al.* *v.* State of Maryland, Use of Pottle, 18 How. 396.

[5] Crowther's Case, Cro. Eliz. 654.

an assault committed in his presence, as is stated in § 314, *ante*, escapes, the justice of the peace may order a constable to pursue and retake the offender without a warrant. The justice of the peace has the same authority to command assistance in pursuing and retaking an offender whom he has caused to be arrested for an offence committed in his presence and who has escaped, that he has to command assistance in making the original arrest.[1]

§ 317. Powers of determination and action of a *quasi* judicial character are given to justices of the peace by the statute referred to in § 314, *ante*, which from their nature must be exercised finally and conclusively, without a hearing or even notice to the parties who may be affected.[2]

§ 318. Whoever, being required by a justice of the peace, upon view of a breach of the peace or of any other offence proper for his cognizance, to apprehend the offender, refuses or neglects to obey such justice, is subject to punishment by imprisonment for not more than one month or by a fine of not more than fifty dollars; and no person to whom such justice is known or declares himself to be a justice of the peace may plead any excuse on pretence of ignorance of his office.[3]

§ 319. If twelve or more persons, being armed

1 Com. *v.* McGahey, 11 Gray, 194.

2 Salem *v.* Eastern Railroad Co., 98 Mass. 431.

3 R. L. ch. 210, § 32.

with clubs or other dangerous weapons, or if thirty or more persons, whether armed or not, are unlawfully, riotously or tumultuously assembled in a city or town, every justice of the peace living in any such city or town, is required to go among the persons so assembled, or as near to them as may be with safety, and in the name of the Commonwealth command all persons so assembled immediately and peaceably to disperse; and if they do not thereupon immediately and peaceably disperse, each of said justices is required to command the assistance of all persons there present in suppressing such riot or unlawful assembly and arresting such persons.[1]

§ 320. A justice of the peace who, having notice of any such riotous or tumultuous and unlawful assembly in the city or town in which he lives, neglects or refuses immediately to proceed to the place of such assembly, or as near thereto as he can with safety, or omits or neglects to exercise the authority conferred upon him by chapter 211 of the Revised Laws, for suppressing such assembly and for arresting the offenders, may be punished by a fine of not more than three hundred dollars.[2]

§ 321. If any persons who are so riotously or unlawfully assembled, and who have been commanded to disperse, as before provided, refuse or neglect to disperse without unnecessary delay, any two justices of the peace or one justice of the peace,

[1] R. L. ch. 211, § 1. [2] R. L. ch. 211, § 3.

together with a sheriff of the county or his deputy, or in a city the mayor or an alderman, and in a town a selectman, may require the aid of a sufficient number of persons, in arms or otherwise as may be necessary, and may proceed, in such manner as in their judgment is expedient, forthwith to disperse and suppress such assembly, and seize and secure the persons composing the same, so that they may be proceeded with according to law.[1]

§ 322. If, by reason of the efforts made by any two or more of the magistrates or officers named in the foregoing section, or by their direction to disperse such assembly, or to seize and secure the persons composing the same who have refused to disperse, though the number remaining may be less than twelve, any such person or any other person then present is killed or wounded, the magistrates and officers, and all persons acting by their order or under their directions, will be held guiltless, and fully justified in law; and if any of said magistrates or officers, or any person acting under or by their direction, is killed or wounded, all persons so assembled, and all other persons who, when commanded or required, refused to aid and assist said magistrates or officers, will be held answerable therefor.[2]

[1] R. L. ch. 211, § 4.
[2] R. L. ch. 211, § 6.

NOT TO BUY CERTAIN DEMANDS FOR COLLECTION.

§ 323. A justice of the peace who, directly or indirectly, buys or is interested in buying, or, directly or indirectly, lends or advances or agrees to lend or advance any money or other goods, or gives or promises any valuable consideration whatever to any person, as an inducement to place or in consideration of having placed in the hands of any person any bond, note, book-debt or right of action for collection, with intent to make for himself any gain from the fees arising from such collection by legal proceedings, is liable, for each offence, to forfeit not less than twenty nor more than five hundred dollars.[1]

DETERMINATION OF AMOUNT DUE FOR EQUITY OF REDEMPTION.

§ 324. When lands or rights are taken and set off or sold on execution, the debtor may in all cases cause the amount due for redemption to be ascertained at his own expense by three justices of the peace in the manner following: one of the justices is to be chosen by the debtor, one by the creditor, and the third by the two first chosen; or if the creditor neglects to choose one, the justice chosen by the debtor will appoint the other two. After a hearing before the three justices, they or

[1] R. L. ch. 166, § 7.

two of them must make and sign a certificate of the amount which they adjudge to be due for the redemption of the land, which certificate will be final and conclusive between the parties. A tender by the debtor of the amount so adjudged to be due will be a sufficient tender notwithstanding any previous tender.[1]

HABEAS CORPUS.

§ 325. Whoever is imprisoned or restrained of his liberty may, as of right and of course, prosecute a writ of *habeas corpus*, according to the provisions of chapter 191 of the Revised Laws, to obtain relief from such imprisonment or restraint, if it proves to be unlawful, unless:

First, he has been committed for treason or felony, or on suspicion thereof, or as accessory before the fact to a felony, and the cause has been plainly expressed in the warrant of commitment.

Second, he has been convicted or is in execution upon legal process, civil or criminal.

Third, he has been committed on mesne process in a civil action in which he was liable to arrest and imprisonment, unless excessive and unreasonable bail was required.[2] The writ of *habeas corpus* may be granted in poor debtor proceedings.[3]

§ 326. The writ may be issued, irrespective of

[1] R. L. ch. 178, § 34.
[2] R. L. ch. 191, § 1.
[3] R. L. ch. 168, § 72.

the county in which the person is imprisoned or restrained, by a justice of the peace if there is no judge of the supreme judicial court, of the superior court, or of a probate, police, district or municipal court, who is known to said justice of the peace to be within five miles of the place where the party is imprisoned or restrained.[1]

§ 327. When a writ of *habeas corpus* is issued by a justice of the peace, it should appear on the face of the writ, or else on the face of the petition when it is annexed to the writ, that the case exists in which authority is given to a justice of the peace to issue the writ. That is, it should appear that no judge of the supreme or superior court, or of a probate, police, district or municipal court is known to the justice of the peace to be within five miles of the place where the party is imprisoned or restrained.[2]

§ 328. The petition for the writ must be in writing, signed and sworn to by the person for whose release it is intended, or by a person in his behalf, and must state by whom and where the person is imprisoned or restrained, the name of the prisoner and of the person detaining him, if their names are known, or a description of them, if their names are not known, and the cause or pretence of such imprisonment or restraint, according to the knowledge and belief of the petitioner. If the imprisonment

[1] R. L. ch. 191, § 2.
[2] Com. *v.* Moore, 19 Pick. 339.

or restraint is by virtue of a warrant or other process, a copy thereof must be annexed, unless it appears that such copy has been demanded and refused or that, for a sufficient reason, a demand therefor could not be made.[1]

§ 329. The justice of the peace to whom the petition is presented is required, without delay, to issue a writ of *habeas corpus*, substantially in the form heretofore established and used in this Commonwealth, and returnable forthwith to the supreme judicial court, or a justice thereof, at such place as shall be designated in the writ.[2]

§ 330. If the imprisonment or restraint is not by a sheriff, deputy sheriff or jailer, the writ will be in the following form: —

COMMONWEALTH OF MASSACHUSETTS.

To the sheriffs of our several counties and to their respective deputies, *Greeting:*

We command you that the body of , of , by , of , imprisoned and restrained of his liberty, as it is said, you take and have before , a justice of our supreme judicial court at immediately after the receipt of this writ, to do and receive what our said justice shall then and there consider concerning him in this behalf; and summon said then and there to appear before our said justice to show the cause of the taking and detaining of said ; and have you there this writ with your doings thereon.

[1] R. L. ch. 191, § 3. [2] R. L. ch. 191, § 4.

Witness my hand at , this day of
in the year nineteen hundred and .

Justice of the Peace.

The writ must be signed by the justice of the peace issuing it, and may be served in any county by a sheriff or deputy sheriff thereof or of any other county.[1]

§ 331. If the prisoner is detained for a cause or crime for which he is bailable, he is to be admitted to bail if sufficient bail is offered; and if not, he must be remanded with an order of the court or justice expressing the amount in which he is to be held to bail and the court at which he is required to appear; and any justice of the peace authorized to admit to bail may, at any time before the sitting of said court, bail the prisoner pursuant to such order.[2]

INSOLVENCY PROOFS.

§ 332. A justice of the peace or special commissioner may take proofs in insolvency. The creditor in person, or if he is disabled by absence from the Commonwealth, illness or other cause from proving his claim, his agent or attorney testifying to the best of his knowledge and belief, must make an oath before the justice of the peace or special commissioner in substance as follows: —

[1] R. L. ch. 191, § 5, 6.

[2] R. L. ch. 191, § 19; cf. ch. 169, § 4.

I, , do swear that , of , by [*or* against] whom proceedings in insolvency have been instituted, at and before the date of such proceedings was and still is justly and truly indebted to me in the sum of , for which sum or any part thereof I have not, nor has any other person to my use, to my knowledge or belief, received any security or satisfaction whatever, beyond what has been disposed of agreeably to law. And I do further swear that said claim was not procured by me for the purpose of influencing the proceedings in this case. And I do further swear that I have not directly or indirectly made or entered into any bargain, arrangement or agreement, express or implied, to sell, transfer or dispose of my claim, or any part of my claim, against said debtor, nor have directly or indirectly received or taken, or made or entered into any bargain, arrangement, or agreement, express or implied, to take or receive directly or indirectly any money, property, or consideration whatsoever to myself, or to any person or persons to my use or benefit, under or with any understanding or agreement, express or implied, whereby my vote for assignee or my assent to the debtor's discharge is or shall be in any way affected, influenced, or controlled, or whereby the proceedings in this case are or shall be affected, influenced or controlled.[1]

INSPECTION OF DRUGGISTS' BOOKS AS TO LIQUOR SALES, ETC.

§ 333. Justices of the peace, in all cities and towns having no licensing boards, may inspect

[1] R. L. ch. 163, §§ 39, 40, 41.

druggists' books, certificates and prescriptions of sales of intoxicating liquor, and the books of dealers in paints or in chemicals licensed to sell pure alcohol.[1]

LIMITED PARTNERSHIP ACKNOWLEDGMENTS.

§ 334. A justice of the peace or special commissioner may take acknowledgments of limited partnership certificates. The certificate should be acknowledged by all the partners.[2]

SOLEMNIZATION OF MARRIAGE.

§ 335. A marriage may be solemnized in any place within this Commonwealth by a justice of the peace if he is also clerk or assistant clerk of a city or town, or a registrar or assistant registrar, in the city or town in which he holds such office, or if he is also clerk or assistant clerk of a court, in the city or town in which the court is authorized to be held, or if he has been designated as stated in the following section and has received a certificate of designation and has qualified thereunder, in the city or town in which he resides; but no person may solemnize a marriage in this Commonwealth unless he is able to read and write the English language.[3]

§ 336. The governor may in his discretion desig-

[1] R. L. ch. 100, §§ 26, 27, 32.

[2] R. L. ch. 71, § 5; cf. ch. 17, § 5 (see § 205, *ante*).

[3] R. L. ch. 151, § 30.

nate a justice of the peace in each city and town and such further number, not exceeding one for every five thousand inhabitants of a city or town, as he considers expedient, to solemnize marriages, and may for cause at any time revoke such designation. The secretary of the Commonwealth will, upon payment of five dollars to him by a justice of the peace so designated, issue to him a certificate of such designation.[1]

§ 337. Every justice of the peace must make and keep a record of each marriage solemnized by him, and of all facts relative to the marriage which are required by law to be recorded.[2] These facts are, the date of the record, the date of the marriage, the place of the marriage, the name, residence and official station of the justice by whom it was solemnized, the names and places of birth of the parties married, the residence of each, the age and color of each, the number of the marriage (as the first or second), and if previously married, whether widowed or divorced, the occupation of each and the names of their parents, and the maiden names of the mothers. If the woman is a widow or divorced, her maiden name must also be given.[3]

§ 338. The justice must also, between the first and tenth days of the month following each marriage solemnized by him, return each certificate to the clerk or registrar who issued the same; and

[1] R. L. ch. 151, § 31. [2] R. L. ch. 151, § 32.
[3] R. L. ch. 29, § 1.

if the marriage was solemnized in a city or town other than the place or places in which the parties to the marriage resided, return a copy of the certificate, or of either certificate if two were issued, to the clerk or registrar of the city or town in which the marriage was solemnized. Each certificate and copy so returned must contain a statement giving the place and date of marriage, attested by the signature of the justice of the peace who solemnized the same. The justice who solemnized the marriage must add his title of office by virtue of which the marriage was solemnized, as "justice of the peace," and his residence. All certificates or copies so returned are recorded by the clerk or registrar who receives them. Whoever neglects to make the record and returns required is liable to forfeit not less than twenty nor more than one hundred dollars.[1]

§ 339. If a certificate of marriage is found, upon its return to the clerk or registrar, to have been incorrectly filled out by the justice of the peace who solemnized a marriage under it, the clerk or registrar must have it corrected and is required to enforce the penalties, if any, provided by law relative thereto. Such imperfect certificates are to be recorded and indexed by the clerk or registrar.[2]

§ 340. A marriage which is solemnized by a person who professes to be a justice of the peace will

[1] R. L. ch. 151, § 32. [2] R. L. ch. 151, § 33.

not be void, nor will the validity thereof be in any way affected by want of authority in such person, or by an omission or by informality in the manner of entering the intention of marriage, if the marriage is in other respects lawful and is consummated with a full belief of either of the persons so married that they have been lawfully married.[1]

§ 341. A city by ordinance and a town by vote may authorize its clerk or registrar to pay on demand, in his office, twenty-five cents to any justice of the peace who has legally solemnized a marriage in this Commonwealth, after the receipt by such clerk or registrar of the certificate in legal form of the solemnization of such marriage.[2]

EVIDENCE OF MARRIAGE.

§ 342. The record of a marriage made and kept as provided by law by the justice of the peace by whom the marriage was solemnized, or a copy of such record duly certified, is made *prima facie* evidence of such marriage.[3]

PENALTIES.

§ 343. Whoever, not being duly authorized by the statutes of this Commonwealth, undertakes to join persons in marriage in this Commonwealth may be punished by a fine of not more than

[1] R. L. ch. 151, § 34.
[2] R. L. ch. 151, § 36.
[3] R. L. ch. 151, § 37.

five hundred dollars or by imprisonment for not more than one year, or by both such fine and imprisonment.[1]

§ 344. If a justice of the peace, being duly authorized to solemnize marriages in this Commonwealth, joins in marriage persons who have not complied with the statutes relative to procuring certificates of notice of intention of marriage, he may be punished by a fine of not more than five hundred dollars.[2]

§ 345. A justice of the peace, though duly authorized to solemnize marriages, may not do so if he has reasonable cause to believe that the male is under the age of twenty-one years or the female is under the age of eighteen years, except with the consent of the parent or guardian having the custody of the minor, if there is any such parent or guardian in this Commonwealth competent to act. Whoever violates this provision may upon conviction within one year after such violation be punished by a fine of not more than five hundred dollars or by imprisonment for not more than one year, or by both such fine and imprisonment.[3]

FEES FOR SOLEMNIZING MARRIAGES.

§ 346. The statutory fee for lawfully solemnizing and certifying a marriage is one dollar and twenty-five cents.[4]

[1] R. L. ch. 151, § 40.
[2] R. L. ch. 151, § 41.
[3] R. L. ch. 151, §§ 7, 40, 43.
[4] R. L. ch. 204, § 26.

ANNUAL LIST OF DESIGNATED JUSTICES.

§ 347. A list of all justices of the peace designated to solemnize marriages under the provisions of the Revised Laws, as stated in § 336, *ante*, with the dates of expiration of their commissions, and notice of any revocation of a designation shall be sent annually in January to the city and town clerks and registrars by the secretary of the Commonwealth.[1]

NOMINATIONS OF GUARDIANS.

§ 348. The nomination of a guardian by a minor above the age of fourteen years may be made before a justice of the peace or special commissioner, who must certify the fact to the probate court.[2]

REMOVAL OF GATES, ETC., ON TOWN AND PRIVATE WAYS.

§ 349. Any person may remove gates, rails, bars or fences which are upon or across a highway, town way or private way legally laid out, or they may be removed by the order of a justice of the peace, unless they have been placed there to prevent the spread of a disease dangerous to the public health, or unless they have been erected or continued by the license of the county commission-

[1] R. L. ch. 5, § 9.

[2] R. L. ch. 145, § 3.

ers, or of the selectmen or road commissioners or of the person for whose use such private way was laid out.[1]

§ 350. The power conferred upon justices of the peace to order fences, gates, rails or bars across highways, town ways or private ways to be removed, is no more a judicial power than if it had been vested in the selectmen or in the surveyors of highways, or than is the power which any citizen has to remove like obstructions. This not being a judicial power, an order of a justice of the peace for the removal of such an obstruction is not in the nature of a judicial warrant, and the sheriff or his deputy is not required in his official capacity to serve it.[2]

INSPECTION OF PEDLERS' LICENSES.

§ 351. Justices of the peace may command pedlers to exhibit to them their licenses. The licenses are granted for the term of one year by the secretary of the Commonwealth; they must contain the names of the cities and towns which the pedler selects, with the sums to be paid to the respective treasurers; they may be granted for the sale of any goods, wares or merchandise, except jewelry, wines, spirituous liquors and playing cards. The sale of these by pedlers is prohibited.[3]

[1] R. L. ch. 53, § 3. [2] Davis *v.* Smith, 130 Mass. 113.
[3] R. L. ch. 65, § 25; cf. ibid., §§ 13, 14, 19, 23.

WITNESSES.

§ 352. A justice of the peace or a special commissioner may issue summonses for witnesses in all cases pending before courts, magistrates, auditors, referees, arbitrators or other persons authorized to examine witnesses; but a justice of the peace or special commissioner may not issue summonses for witnesses in criminal cases except upon the request of the attorney-general, district attorney or other person who acts in the case in behalf of the Commonwealth or of the defendant. If the summons is issued at the request of the defendant that fact must be stated therein. The summons shall be in the form heretofore adopted and commonly used, but may be altered from time to time like other writs. No person is required to attend as a witness in a civil case or for the defendant in a criminal case, unless the fees allowed by law for one day's attendance and for travel to and from the place where he is required to attend are paid or tendered to him.[1]

Form of Subpœna.

COMMONWEALTH OF MASSACHUSETTS.

[Name of County] } ss.

To A. B. of T., in the county of E., and within said Commonwealth, *Greeting:*

You are hereby required, in the name of the Commonwealth of Massachusetts, to appear before the

[1] R. L. ch. 175, §§ 1, 3.

court , holden at , within and for the county of , on the day of , at o'clock in the noon, and from day to day thereafter, until the action hereinafter named is heard by said court, to give evidence of what you know relating to an action of then and there to be heard and tried between C. D. of M., in the county of S. and within said Commonwealth, plaintiff, and E. F. of said M., defendant [*If a subpœna with duces tecum is desired, add*, and you are further required to bring with you (*here state what, if any, books, papers, etc., must be brought*).].

Hereof fail not, as you will answer your default under the pains and penalties in the law in that behalf made and provided.

Dated at B. the day of , A. D. 190 .

S. P.,
Justice of the Peace.
[or *Special Commissioner.*]

§ 353. The fee of a justice of the peace or special commissioner for a subpœna for one or more witnesses is ten cents.[1]

PENALTY FOR FORGING DOCUMENTS OF JUSTICES, ETC.

§ 354. Whoever, with intent to injure or defraud, falsely makes, alters, forges or counterfeits a certificate, return or attestation of a justice of the peace or any other public officer, in relation to a

[1] R. L. ch. 204, § 1.

matter wherein such certificate, return or attestation may be received as legal proof, or whoever with such intent utters and publishes as true such false, forged or altered instrument, knowing the same to be so, is liable to punishment by imprisonment in the state prison for not more than ten years or in jail for not more than two years.[1]

[1] R. L. ch. 209, § 1, 3.

INDEX.

INDEX.

Spotted something that isn't quite right?

Let us know and we'll fix it for future reprints.
And as a thank you for your diligence, we'll
send you a free Sothis book of your choice.

publisher@sothis.press

This page intentionally left blank

Except of course for that line above. And this one.
And whilst we have your attention, perhaps you'd
like to follow us on Instagram @sothis.press. Go on.

Made in the USA
Monee, IL
08 November 2026

68113591R00166